1986

N

# WHEN YOUR NAME
# IS ON THE DOOR

# When Your Name Is on the Door

## Earl D. Brodie

BOOKS IN FOCUS  NEW YORK

Manufactured in the United States Of America


Books in Focus, Inc.
P.O. Box 3481
Grand Central Station
New York, New York 10163


**Library of Congress Cataloging in Publication Data**
Brodie, Earl D      1918-
    When your name is on the door.
    Includes index.
    1. Small business—Management. I. Title.
HD62. 7. B76    1981    658' .022      80-66756
ISBN   0-916728-45-5

In memory of
RALPH N. BRODIE
Whose Name Was on the Door First

Although some of the material pertaining to international economics in Chapters V and VI is based upon articles written by Mr. William H. Tehan for *Newsletter For Independent Businessowners,* I am completely responsible for everything in those chapters as well as everything in this book.

# Contents

ONE
**What This Book—and You—are About  3**

TWO
**You are Different  23**

THREE
**When Your Name is on the Note  37**

FOUR
**Arise, Prisoners of Starvation  51**

FIVE
**The Economic Ocean in Which
  We Swim  71**

SIX
**Bigger Fish in the Sea  81**

SEVEN
## Housekeeping for Businessowners    101

EIGHT
## Free Enterprise for Who?    127

NINE
## How Does It Feel to be Perfect?    149

TEN
## Truman's Half Truth    163

ELEVEN
## Hiring the Help    179

TWELVE
## Handling the Help    193

THIRTEEN
## Firing the Help    223

FOURTEEN
## Your Son, Your Son    237

FIFTEEN
## When Your Name is off the Door    249

INDEX    263

# WHEN YOUR NAME IS ON THE DOOR

# CHAPTER ONE

# What This Book —and You— are About

You run your own business. The union wants more. Is that a problem of employee or labor relations? More money, or they'll strike. How can you decide how much to pay without looking at your hole card—lower right hand corner of the balance sheet?

So is it a financial problem? How can you think about your stake without going back to the top section straight across— your receivables and payables?

So is it simply a matter of current assets and liabilities? But where will you be next month and next year?

Over to the operating statement. Sales. And what do you project for next year? Has the union situation become a marketing problem? And what about competition?

You've gone through this many times. Suppose the opening question was what to do when your competitor cuts prices? Or suppliers aren't supplying? Or while one government bureau demands that you put out dollars to comply with its regulations, another bureau threatens you with jail if you do, and your lawyer can't understand either one? Is that a regulatory or strictly financial question? You're going to make a bet, based on probabilities.

Round and round the Independent Businessowner goes.

Because your business is not—as the private sector bureaucrats who baby-sit the huge public corporations that nobody really owns, and the professors of business administration who have never owned a business to administer, would have it—a collection of separate functions, or departments. It's a single sack of snakes, affording no way to attack one "problem" without thinking about the whole shebang.

Just like a doctor will not put you under a general anesthetic to set a broken foot without first checking your blood pressure and assorted other manifestations of your total body performance.

An independent business may not be as complicated as the chemistry of the human body, but runs it a close second with respect to the way everything is wound up in everything else.

And that's the reason *When Your Name Is on the Door* is not divided into artificial sections—textbook fashion—that attempt to tell you how to handle each function as if you were in a classroom presided over by a professor of industrial relations who seems unaware of the fact that the firm's goods must be sold.

Now don't get upset. This is not one long dithyramb. To make them easy to read, my conclusions on what to do in the independent business are chopped into chapters. Each will emphasize one aspect of deciding what to do, but will send offshoots to other related considerations.

But don't expect me to sacrifice the book's central message—that Independent Businessowners must run their business for selfish motives only, deciding what to do in all matters by that standard—on the altar of the academic fiction that the various responsibilities and duties of the owner can be considered separately.

I suspect a fellow would need a Ph.D. from a graduate

school of business administration to do a job like that, and I don't have one. In fact, it's doubtful I could ever have been admitted to such an institution. In spite of this ghastly defect in my background, however, my balance sheet is in pretty fair shape.

Besides, I am writing just for businessowners and nobody else. And about figuring out what to do. I'm not going to insult your intelligence by telling you how to do things.

If I offend pompous professors or nail-biting private sector politicians who spend their dreary lives looking over their shoulders in companies selling for less than book value, that's too damn bad.

In any event, they have no business reading this, although a few will probably sneak in. As I say, this book is intended for Independent Businessowners only, who have their own way of looking at things and deciding what to do. True of any racket. Just as police detectives, pimps, prostitutes and politicians all have their lingo, clubs, and unspoken understandings among themselves and within their own groups, so do we businessowners.

We're all in the same boat — regardless whether we started, bought, inherited, or stole the business — afloat on a gummy sea called the international political economy, over which we could have some control if we wanted to go get it. As to the competitive winds created by big business, it's just a matter of proper setting of sails to plow ahead. While a business idea is plodding through the chain-of-command and committee meat grinder of a major corporation, you can — and do — decide what to do, and do it.

Nor do the employees of the business giants — specifically including Presidents and Chairmen — have the nerve, guts, motivation, willingness to work, determination, or sense of a buck that you have. They're job-holders who have to ask for a raise.

You're different. Because you have created a totally different situation for yourself. After all, who is going to give you a Christmas bonus? Or maybe just a turkey?

Your answer establishes your unique position in our political economy better than 40 pages of explanation.

Business owners are different because they are the only people in the country who are 100 percent responsible for their own living . . . and their own destiny. You stand or fall by your personal efforts.

The late, and for some unfathomable reason now semi-sainted Harry Truman was no more truthful than usual when he said, "the buck stops here." He blamed Congress for his troubles. Called it a "do-nothing Congress."

Everything in your shop is your responsibility. Including the things that happen when you're not there.

Why remind you of this? Because businessowners are frequently distracted into thinking like employees by friends, seminar leaders, and business writers who themselves are employees. Sometimes getting six-figure salaries with commensurate perks. But someone else gives them a raise or bonus.

As employees, they carry out decisions made by others. When they in turn make decisions, such action is still within the framework of duties that have been assigned to them.

As a result, these folks are usually serious students of something called "management." Freely translated, the term means figuring out how to please the boss. Not unreasonable, when you have a boss.

If your business is big enough to support one or more managers, don't hesitate to turn them loose on figuring out how to organize work, judge subordinate employees, etc. after you have decided what is to be done.

And that's the key to your success. Deciding what to do. That's where your attention must be. Using pencil or calculator. How much of what to buy? For what delivery? On what terms? Pricing with respect to cost and market. It's impossible to review these kinds of numbers too often.

You'll make more money using your brains on those and related matters than by rushing around the shop or field putting out fires. That's what employees are for.

Remember, you are not "management." You are the owner. Because you are the owner, books that purportedly tell you how to run your business are useless to you. Look at your bookshelves. You've bought dozens of such books, tried to read them, and given up.

Not that they were badly written. Probably the authors — usually school teachers in the higher grades — all have a better command of English than I do.

The reason you stopped reading was that you already know how to run your business. You do it your way. The publishers who lost money on these tomes failed to recognize that running a business is a very personal thing. Like pulling your socks on. Or combing your hair. No two people do it exactly the same way.

What you ask when you go to your counselor-consultant, CPA, attorney, or bartender — is for some idea as to what to do.

It is impossible to teach anyone to make money running a business.

It is possible to teach accounting (keeping records for people who do make money), engineering (designing things that can't be made at competitive prices), advertising (convincing clients you are brilliant without increasing their volume), purchasing (spending money made by others), and personnel management (spending still more money earned by others).

In making money, there is only your way, the way that works for you. The modern, sickening expression is the way you are "comfortable." Who cares? What's a little discomfort if you're raking in the dough?

In most categories of work, there are probably right and wrong ways to get things done.

Schools of business administration teach how to administer the affairs of men who are making money.

This book is strictly for people who own their own businesses, and run them for their personal benefit. It is not for employees, no matter how large their salaries.

The inside front cover of *Business Week* for December 31, 1979 consisted of a beautiful ad by Control Data headed, "The Business of Business is to Address the Major Needs of Society."

That may be the business of Control Data, but it is exactly

the opposite of the business of the Independent Businessowner. To the extent that he believes such claptrap, the Independent Businessowner is economically castrating himself.

Just among us businessowners, let's admit that the purpose of your business is to provide as high a standard of living and as much security as possible for yourself and those dependent upon you. Period.

Now, if you want to label selling drill presses to machine shops or merchandising candy bars and toothpaste to drugstore customers as addressing a major need of society, go to it. But if you do, remember it's a private joke.

The greatest threat to the Independent Businessowner in this country, believe it or not, is neither the government, the unions, nor competition of major companies—especially not competition from major companies, because most of them don't know how to compete.

The major threat is the mistaken idea that he has any purpose for being in business other than to make some dough.

Now, after you've made your money, if you want to donate it to the Society for Homeless Goldfish or to any other worthy cause, that's your affair. It's your dough and you can do what you want with it, but don't get that confused with the whole point of being in business.

Similarly, if you teach some employees to do things in such a way that they eventually get better jobs or start businesses of their own, well and good. That's an expense you had to incur for your own benefit. Just as you learned some things working for other people and are glad that there's no way anybody— not even the government—can take away what is in your head or your hands, bear in mind that your former employer was not in business to teach school. Neither are you. Teaching is an expense, not a contribution.

So don't let advertising copy-writers who serve the huge companies that nobody really owns, or "industrial statesmen" who have inherited so much money that they give it away to leftwing causes and candidates, distract you into thinking you have any business objective other than raking in all you can.

If you're looking for a book of standard forms or procedures, the library is full of them. We're less concerned with how to do things than we are with the principal question of the Independent Businessowner, which is what to do in order to make money for himself.

Besides, telling others how to do things is usually a waste of energy. The main objective is to be sure that businessowners know what to do. Once that is clearly in mind — and by the normal course of events through the owner's head and into the heads of employees — the how part comes easy.

For example, if you want an employee to go from Chicago to New York the fastest way on a clear spring day, you don't have to tell him that he must use an airplane. On the other hand, if you want him to travel from San Francisco to Los Angeles on sudden notice, the day before Christmas and the weather is lousy, if you have to tell him to drive, you should have fired him a long time ago.

So, stated another way, the purpose of this book is to enable you, the Independent Businessowner, to see yourself correctly as the unique individual you are — philosophically, politically, economically.

Once an Independent Businessowner understands his true situation he is better able to make business decisions for business reasons. Know what he is doing.

A business reason is one designed to make money. For example, the owner of a factory moved to a new industrial park and built a costly plant to please his pride. He would have been financially ahead by expanding at the old location and/or putting on another shift.

This book will make it easier for any Independent Businessowner to acknowledge that whatever silly reason he originally had for going into business — notions about markets for hootnannies, ego, got fired — his only reason for staying in business now is to make money. Neglect of that principle starts him on the path to oblivion.

Most books for businessowners are devoted to the mechanics of the job, such as production engineering, marketing, personnel procedures, accounting controls, insurance, traffic management, purchasing techniques, etc. Not much different from standard texts on these subjects for corporate employees. *When Your Name Is on the Door* gets to the philosophical basis of business ownership.

It is very different from working as a highly paid executive — that is to say, employee. Ownership is not management.

The Independent Businessowner has hang-ups, and sometimes is made to feel guilty. *When Your Name Is on the Door* will make you feel good about yourself, proud of your status. Clear your mind by washing out emotional cobwebs that interefere with making money.

As I said earlier, *When Your Name Is on the Door* is not for outsiders. Especially it is not for so-called professional managers — private sector bureaucrats who can't get a raise or promotion without working at company politics. Maybe that's what's wrong with the stock market.

*When Your Name Is on the Door* will clarify the role of the Independent Businessowner by contrasting it with the so-called professional managers mentioned above. In doing so, it will probably be necessary to murder some sacred cows, blast many myths of management, and show that while they might be good guidance for career bootlickers, they have nothing to do with running a business.

Management is a job. Ownership is a way of thinking.

Our accurately named schools of business administration seem to be organized on the unstated assumption that everyone will go to work for someone else. And they're probably right, as far as their students are concerned. You can teach youngsters how to administer a business nobody really owns, but you can't teach anyone how to make money. So their alumni become life-long employees, and probably vote Democratic.

Let's elaborate on this. Not long ago I had lunch with the No. 3 man in an NYSE firm. With pride, he related how No. 1 had called him in, told him what a great job he was doing, and indicated that if he could just do thus-and-so he'd be in line for a fat raise. No. 3 was really happy. His efforts to play to No. 1's ideas were paying off.

But the amazing thing is that this man has a six-figure salary. And a total employee mentality to match. Boss-oriented. Has to play to a superior . . . to his boss's boss. (Expensive seminars are offered on this subject by "management" organizations.)

But who gives a businessowner a raise? That's one way you're different from the corporate executive.

And since nothing can be done in a large organization controlled by its employees except by trading favors — like log-rolling in congress — the operatives are not merely playing politics. They are full-time politicians.

You, as owner, do not decide what to do based on how you expect another politician to react. But it's easy to slip into the political mode because so many of your friends work for companies, and practically all "business" writing is by them — or their ghost writers — or is aimed at them.

Independent Businessowners who base their decisions on their own balance sheets and markets make an excellent living, put a little aside, and will survive the economic and political purgatory being prepared for us by our politicians.

Independent Businessowners who are dazzled by the slick lingo — it's really supposed to be sophisticated management talk — of the caretakers of the huge corporations that nobody really owns may not be with us when the dust and smoke clear away.

Before you take them seriously, or regard major company executives as outstanding models after whom to pattern your policies and actions, consider the following from an article by Dr. Carl H. Madden, Professor of Business and Government Relations at the American University, that appeared in *Enterprise*, published by NAM:

"By 2008 the public would evaluate corporations by . . . social performance in traditional markets . . . in 'public needs' markets . . . in non-economic values deemed important by society.

" . . . a new definition of efficiency will . . . include accounting for the cost of production involving health, safety, and environmental impact . . . Manufacturing . . . will likely be shifting to underdeveloped areas in the country and the world.

" . . . corporations will . . . direct their business action . . . to achieve social objectives such as equality of opportunity, management of natural resources, development of human resources . . .

" . . . Events are moving in a direction exactly opposite to the doctrine that corporations should limit their activities to classic profit making."

The alarming thing is that the good professor is probably right. Judging from the principal activity of the supervisory employees who administer public companies, who devote more attention to internal politics and "maintaining relations" with their comrades in government than to making money, they are preparing their juniors for exclusively bureaucratic roles.

Of course, history might get a small nudge from the AFL-CIO regarding that business of moving manufacturing to underdeveloped countries!

Nor is this acknowledged not-for-profit attitude likely to bull the stock market.

The significance of this to Independent Businessowners is twofold:

First, if any of you still view these corporate fuglemen as worthy of emulation, it's time to forget that and look for the profit in every deal. Your job is to buy low, sell high, and keep your expenses down, while keeping an eye on your markets and on your real strength as expressed by the balance sheet.

The executives who pontificate, give interviews, and testify before legislative committees like to give the impression of being all-knowing. Magazine and financial-page editors whose salaries depend on advertising placed by them show little enthusiasm for deflating their egos.

So we smaller fry are influenced by them, based on the

unstated assumption that such august personages must be very successful businessmen indeed. Perhaps, but even so, they are in all cases first proven politicians whose records are written on a track paved with cost-plus government contacts. And if such a man flops in one company, his former directors, assisted by an obliging head hunter, will fix him up with another after the government bails him out. Directors who know that he has a pretty good map of certain graveyards.

In exception to this are men like Al Rockwell and Henry Ford who have truly built their companies. Both their firms used to be independently owned. Strange how it makes a difference — regardless of the size of the operation — when it's your name that's on the door!

Some businessowners read "management" books, mostly written by academics speaking for multinationals. Fortunately, not as many read as buy them, judging from the volumes I see collecting dust in clients' offices.

Most of this is mental poison to the Independent Businessowner. If you feel a need to improve your mind by reading, consider Shakespeare. Since most of our troubles are caused by ourselves, at least Shakespeare offers insight into human cussedness.

The second way in which the fact that big business is halfway down the primrose path to socialism is significant to businessowners, is that it underlines the important of hanging on to the business. The business you own will continue to be a better investment than any stock you buy. The listed firms, based on Dr. Madden's well-supported scenario, will — in terms of actual buying power — pay diminishing dividends.

And as to loaning money to the government or corporations — that's called "buying bonds" — the value of your asset fluctuates with interest rates.

Does this contradict advice elsewhere in the book that the Independent Businessowner wants to be able to get his dough out of the pickle works? No. Because by maintaining the kind of balance sheet that would attract buyers, you'll make money now and be able to sell out at a decent figure should age, family, or estate planning make that the right decision down the road.

So, with respect to Madden's article, start thinking as your grandfather did, not as your grandson will have to.

Independent Businessowners make money by running their business for that purpose and no other.

Former Independent Businessowners — now entombed in bankruptcy statistics — suffocated in their own overhead and/or hanged themselves on a misconception of their role in life by attempting to imitate the corporation bureaucrats who are destroying their companies' earnings and share values by sleeping with government bureaucrats.

For example, TIME for May 15, 1978 quoted the President of Equitable Life: "To cater only to the maximization of profits is to invite corporate doom."

The article goes on to list the boy scout deeds Equitable has done. Mainly hiring and promoting women and minorities.

Aside from the obvious fact that if such hiring policies load the payroll with second-rate help, the difference for Equitable can be charged off to advertising, be warned that the Independent Businessowner who thinks about anything other than the maximization of profits is inviting his personal economic doom — and fast.

While the private sector politicians who administer the huge insurance companies, banks, and utilities that nobody really owns sometimes give lip service to capitalism, they have no reason to resist a government whose regulations not only relieve them from responsibility for poor earnings, but actually in effect guarantee them a continuous cost-plus business that keeps them in cakes and perks.

To illustrate, have you ever heard a major corporation chairman or president suggest OSHA be abolished?

That evil monstrosity — the most un-American, anti-personal liberty bureau yet created — hatched during an allegedly Republican administration, has landed with all fours not on the conglomerates whose personnel departments welcomed it with the enthusiasm only a bureaucrat who sees a chance to hire more people can muster, but primarily on the Independent Businessowner.

Was it General Motors or Dupont who fought OSHA to the Supreme Court? No, it was an Idaho Independent Businessowner.

And in California, banks and major corporations actually joined their brother bureaucrats in government to oppose Proposition 13.

It's enough to make a fellow believe the rightwing claim that the entire tax and government setup actually is a Marxist plot to destroy the middle class.

So, while my father, who ran a machine shop during the twenties could look at Henry Ford I and say, "If I do like Henry does, maybe I too can build a big business," your son can't figure to build business by emulating the successors of Henry Ford II. Those gentlemen, according to the President of Equitable, will "invite corporate doom by catering only to the maximization of profits."

Your job is to make all business decisions for business reasons. "To maximize profits."

WHAT TO DO:
Disregard the ways and means of public corporations.

Obey the hiring and environmental regulations as best you can. Negotiate with the enforcers as you do with business agents. Be practical. Make the best deals you can. Don't try to prove points.

Why men work is the title of at least one book and the subject of many others.

Why Independent Businessowners work is no mystery. You are working to make money.

Because of the incessant promotion of notions to the contrary, to which you have been subjected, I must again remind you that money is your only motivation. Before you throw up your hands in horror and say absolutely not, take a look at your personal balance sheet and ascertain how much capital you have outside of the business on which you could live if your business ceased to exist. How long would it sustain you?

There is probably more unadulterated nonsense in circulation on this general subject than on any other business matter with the possible exception of employee relations. We'll come to that later.

It's been fashionable for academics and sob-sisters—damn few of whom have ever done any work—to explore the question of why employees at all levels work.

This is usually done through questionnaires that by attempting to ask the same question in various forms, supposedly trap the person responding into revealing his innermost feelings. The idea is to demonstrate that the questionnaires elicit, not simply what a person says is his reason for working, but his real reason. Unfortunately there is no evidence that the questionnaires achieve their tricky objectives.

This idiocy is usually supplemented by interviews conducted by graduate students who believe anything their professors tell them, and/or clipboard-carrying housewives working for less than the minimum wage who haven't the foggiest notion of what they are supposedly doing.

It would be relatively harmless except for the fact that from time to time Independent Businessowners, because of their unwitting tendency to imitate the supervisory employees of larger companies, deceive themselves concerning their reason for being in business.

They may momentarily decide they are working for the "challenge"—or "game"—of the situation, or to discharge some vague social obligation. Another side-stepping idea is that you're in business for the purpose of rendering a service, or to provide opportunities for employees to develop their talents. The old "we're in the people business" gag. As I said a minute ago, more on that awaits you.

There is nothing inherently wrong with giving this type of response to reporters, poll-takers, or journalists who are desperately trying to find something with which to fill up the space between ads for hemorrhoid remedies.

It is hazardous, however, to kid yourself.

Basically, you'll do a better job of running your business if your avowedly selfish motives are clearly and consistently before you. And if you feel vaguely guilty about your profit motive — because you too have been influenced by the socialist philosophy that governs our education and media establishments — think how much fun it would be to go back to work on the bench. Even at today's inflated wages.

And when talking about making money, I don't mean "making money for the company." I'm talking about making money for yourself. If you own the business, an increase in its equity should only be there to expand it in order to make more money, to reduce income taxes if possible, or to fatten it up for eventual sale.

Most of the psychologizing about why men work is centered around employees. They may be ordinary production and clerical workers, or hold highly paid jobs in major corporations.

These writers, interestingly, are smart enough not to interview female workers. The reason is that women make it abundantly clear they are working for dollars, period.

Independent Businessowners, a breed apart, are usually ignored by authors and journalists in this field. Perhaps the would-be interviewers know instinctively that what you might tell them would not fit into their preconceived ideas.

But the fact that you are different from employees does not mean you are omniscient.

Independent Businessowners have usually done everything in the shop.

The resulting trap they set for themselves is the conclusion that they know all about everything, and thereby sacrifice profit on the altar of vanity.

A basic entrepreneurial expertise is that of identifying the skills you lack and hiring employees or outside services that do have them. Neglect of this principle can push you into a tub of red ink.

Here are three examples of such neglect.

1. The prime mover of an olive cooperative had personally handled their promotion from the beginning. One morning he decided a good way to sell his wares would be to give away recipe books, in which all recipes required olives. He received countless requests for the books, but olive sales remained flat.

He then called in an advertising agency known to be successful in promoting foodstuffs. They analyzed the situation and discovered that the books were not selling his product because olives are not a basic ingredient to any recipe. In other words, it's easy to leave them out.

The agency reported this to the client and presented a new — and ultimately successful — program. Months later, however, the executive in charge of the olive account was startled to learn that the co-op was still spending money printing and mailing recipe books because the head honcho liked the book. There was even a low-keyed effort to prevent the agency from finding out!

2. A CPA recently told of a client who was also a good friend. The client had sustained losses he did not relate to the CPA when it was time to prepare tax returns. He was ashamed to inform his friend of his bad judgment. The matter came to light in time for him to get the proper deductions because the accountant was a thorough sort of fellow who went down the list of his client's various securities and asked about the present status of each.

3. A valve manufacturer who engaged an employer association to represent him in negotiating a new union agreement made it clear he would give a maximum increase of thirty cents an hour. If the union insisted on more, he would take a strike. Negotiations continued past the deadline. The negotiator telephoned his client once more to be sure everything was clear. The owner did not change his position. The union struck.

After the men were on the bricks, the owner told the negotiator he shouldn't have had a strike because he was willing to pay another fifteen cents an hour, which in this case would have more than made the difference. He had not revealed his true position because he feared that the negotiator would have given away the entire amount unnecessarily!

What do these events — they all actually occurred — have in common? Decisions based on feelings or emotions rather than rational business thinking.

When you buy labor or service, be sure to get your money's worth!

Not that you should uncritically accept everything employees or outside services offer. Test their ideas. Cross-examine. Then, having determined criteria of acceptance, apply them objectively. Why cheat yourself?

Nor should you negotiate with your negotiators. Make business decisions for business reasons, not out of pride, stubbornness, or the notion that you are a man for all seasons. And don't let your vanity steal your money.

While taking care not to imitate the attitudes of the minions of large organizations, it's also important to recognize another trap at the opposite end of the scale — the trap of doing your employees' work.

For example, a pump manufacturer once told me, "I'm going down to the plant Sunday and muck out my office."

Are you, like him, working as a job holder, rather than as a businessowner?

Are you too judging yourself by the amount of work you do rather than the return you are getting on your investment, based on having made business decisions for business reasons? Have you set up routine chores for yourself which prevent you from running the business?

Here are a few examples of things I have found businessowners doing that have distracted them from their primary responsibility of increasing the return on their investment:

Opening all the mail every morning. Literally.

Signing all checks. Including payroll.

Checking all invoices payable. Also receiving records.

Reviewing every quotation.

All of these things are sometimes justified as providing an overview of the business.

None do. They give you just the opposite—a mouse-eye view.

It's wrong to do employees' work. It's right to check their work.

What are you doing that you could teach an employee to do? (Assuming the particular function needs to be performed at all.)

Are you working like one of your employees because you don't know what to do with yourself? Because there is a limit to the amount of planning, scheduling and checking up of which you are capable?

If so, is there any limit to the direct market investigation and customer contact you have?

Some businessowners engage consultants to study their habits, to ascertain what they are doing all day and then to tell them how to improve. After paying the fees, they still don't change their ways. That's because the ideas came from someone else.

Why not do it yourself? Provided you don't think it will drive you to suicide, every night for two weeks write down your daily activities. Then do two things.

First, study the record and identify the duties and functions that make you no money. Swear on a stack of Bibles that neither you nor any employee will ever again waste time—i.e., your money—on such diversions.

Second, list the functions—probably most of them—you can teach employees to perform. Then do so. You don't get paid for doing their work. The results of your efforts cannot be counted or weighed.

Never again should you be "behind in your work."

Now you are ready to address yourself to the business of putting your dollars where they will earn the most, with due consideration for major economic windstorms and volcanoes—and their effect on your affairs that we'll talk about later.

# CHAPTER TWO

# You are Different

Your name is on the door. That fact in itself makes you different. So don't pretend, or act as if, you are in the same boat as your fellow Republican who is "with" XYZ diaper disposal service.

Notice the polite question is, "Who are you with?" not the "Where do you work?" that one machinist may ask another.

Maybe these so-called executives are too sensitive—"vulnerable" as latter-day sob-sisters say—to admit they are supposed to do any real work.

Your name on the door means, among other things, you'll never take bankruptcy even if you have to clean latrines in one of the less affluent sections of Port Said to pay off.

Nor will it make any difference if you change the name from Francis X. Houlihan Mud Pump Company to Magnificent Mud Pump Company. The creditors will still know it's your pump, your muck, and your obligation. And so will you.

In what other ways are you different?

For one thing, your natural enthusiasm frees you from the artificial calendar barriers and demarcations that govern job-holders. You have the great privilege of regarding every day as New Year's day.

The significance of January 1 is that it is unimportant to Independent Businessowners. Makes you very different.

The trap awaiting you if you pay any special attention to that date is the idea that it will be the only New Year's day you will have during the next 12 months.

Every day is the day to start to develop new products, improve existing ones, or drop others.

Nor did you have to wait until any particular day systematically to reduce costs and expenses, rewrite loan agreements, improve service to present customers and go after new accounts. Every day starts a new period during which something is to be accomplished. Nor are you governed by accounting cycles.

This attitude is different from that of your golfing buddy Wilbur, Vice-President of loose threads down at the ribbon factory. He won't say "Boo" to a goose except through committees, and after judging the probable effect of that terrifying act on his boss's career. Don't be infected by this fear and muddling.

Wilbur wants to be safely committed for a year, which absolves him of thinking. He and his friend Kerfoot down at the Federal Fertilizer Board are like slow trains with steam up and no brakes. They go right down the track, can't deviate right or left, and can't stop until fuel is exhausted.

The Independent Businessowner cages himself by reading so much material which (without saying so) refers to businesses nobody really owns, and then concludes that because of their size they must be run by geniuses worthy of emulation. Not so.

The Independent Businessowner survives by imitating the light-weight boxer, changing directions quickly.

Since to us every day is New Year's day, let's begin on fixed expenses. Maybe they're not all so fixed.

For example, what services do you pay for every month and don't get?

Retainers for intangible services? Advertising? Attorneys? Accountants? Yes, and Management Consultants?

Even the good ones can get lazy once a client starts to pay

the rent. Don't you know anyone more anxious to do the job? Maybe a better job for less money?

Unless any kind of consultant is helping you make money—and you see the dollars coming in or sticking to the cash register at the end of the month—cut off his retainer.

Accumulate questions, and take them up when necessary, at his hourly rate. Or, try a fresh, new expert.

Don't believe that an advertising counselor, lawyer, or consultant's knowledge of your history necessarily makes him more valuable to you than another who comes in cold. It just makes your account more profitable to him.

How many hard questions have you and he answered lately? Have you made any money as a result of these learned colloquies? How do you know?

Turn fixed expenses into variables or eliminate them entirely January 1 and every other day. Every day you get a new chance!

Another way you are different is in your reactions to union gains. That's because it's your dough. But if it's true that executives of the huge corporations that nobody really owns have typical employee attitudes, does it follow that they make a little holiday in their hearts when "forced" to give the union a raise?

Some of them do. Many supervisory employees of large firms, above a certain level, are compensated partly by the profitability of the company after all expenses, including their own and the union's wages have been paid. So there is a crossover point.

Also, some receive stock options, phantom shares, etc. Changes in the tax laws, however, plus the sad record of the stock market during recent years, have made these schemes less attractive than salaries and bonuses.

The only true employers are Independent Businessowners. Men who work for public corporations—including Chairmen and Presidents—are employees.

Anyone who has to ask for a raise—whose compensation is determined by another individual or even a committee—is an employee. And employees can react to business conditions, problems, and opportunities only on their own terms — politically. Because they have nothing at risk, their only question is, "How can this situation help me get a raise or promotion?"

George Meany underscored this in his retirement speech to the AFL-CIO, saying: "The 24 years of merger have proven . . . that all workers share common interests, needs, and expectations regardless of their craft, the color of the collar they wear, or any other artificial distinction."

(Is that why blue shirts are now "in" at the higher levels of big industry?)

So what has this to do with a businessowner trying to decide what to do next?

Everything. Recognizing the importance of taking a fresh look at one's business whenever you remember to, the most important thing to examine is your own state of mind. Your assumptions and objectives.

As that long-ago professor of physics or chemistry taught you, the meat of any science is in its theory, not practice.

By the same token, the important part of the businessowner's job is understanding its true nature, rather than carrying out specific duties. Some owners are so skillful at keeping busy that they manage never to "have time" to think.

To the extent that a businessowner identifies with his golf or bridge-partners — the overpaid private sector bureaucrats who administer big business — he thinks like an employee instead of an owner. Leads to trouble, to thinking in terms of take-home pay and tax-free benefits instead of return on investment.

The objective is return on investment. That's your score as a businessowner. Not how much you keep after taxes. Are you getting as much on your equity as you could get in the bond market, for example?

Are profits staying ahead of inflation? Is the earning power of the business, or the market for its assets increasing to the extent that you or your estate can sell or liquidate to advantage?

Who is representing your industry in Washington? Many trade associations are dominated by employees of large companies that contribute the salary of a 6-figure executive to the association. The benefits he bargains for may do his employer more good than it does the industry or your business.

As an employee, he is also using the opportunity to enhance his own career — maybe find a better job.

The big firms even do it to each other. The most dramatic example is when General Motors did not offer much resistance to the government's costly regulations of the automobile business which Chrysler couldn't afford.

Don't let any major competitor play you for a Chrysler!

You are different because you are never afraid that a subordinate will get your job. In spite of that, Independent Businessowners who boast of having surrounded themselves with men who have skills that they themselves do not possess still only do half a job.

It's easy to say, "I'm a good engineer (chemist, pharmacist, carpenter, mechanic), but I need people skilled in selling and marketing, accounting, etc."

Harder — takes real guts — to say, "I have a silly weakness for buying machines, equipment, or displays that I don't really need. Therefore, my supervisory employees or staff professionals have to restrain me and make sure I justify capital outlays by the pay-out."

It's the personal weaknesses, not the absence of particular skills, that lead a certain number of businessowners to the commercial undertakers every year. Since your fundamental objective is to stay financially afloat, let's take a closer look at five different, daring ways to get more for the money you pay supervisory/administrative employees. We'll cite opposite type actions of corporate officials by contrast.

1. Do you love machines or equipment? Buy them now and figure something will come up later that will enable you to pay them off and make a profit? Or do you like to fight unions or government agencies on matters of principle instead of getting an agreement that will be the least costly?

Corporate managers are likely to be shortsighted in determining the pay-out, or recognizing the types of deals with unions that may seem practical, but establish costly principles.

While it's good strategy to help the union or government official justify his job, the corporation executive crawls into bed with him. They have a lot in common. Both hold their jobs at the pleasure of an electorate of another bureaucrat one notch higher on the totem pole.

WHAT TO DO:

Instruct supervisory/administrative employees to guard you against these—your own weaknesses. Tell them to find justification in numbers, not words—for your capital, labor, and regulatory decisions. Part of their job is to fight you.

That would be suicide for corporate execs. If you compete with major companies, you have a great advantage. You can get more out of your employees.

2. As I have been saying continuously in this treatise—to get it firmly into your mind—the only reason for being in business is to make money. It's clear that many owners did not think this through when they made the plunge. Did you do it for ego? Want your name on the door, although you could make more elsewhere? Don't mind being bossed by hundreds of customers and suppliers, but couldn't take direction from an individual?

As an employee, were you unable to deal with equals? Do you enjoy being on the same footing as others in your club or association now, but had difficulty outside the superior-subordinate relationship in a hierarchy?

Finally—the nuttiest reason for going into business— revenge? Got mad at an employer and entered the field just to show him?

But even if you went into business for wrong reasons, you're there now and so is your money.

What to do?

Unless you started with a written profit plan—practically no one does—figure it now. Your business is your savings and your debt. Any early childish, emotional, or ignorance factors that governed the original decision are no longer important. Nor should they be guiding principles in business decisions

now. Require profit plans from employees who have departments. Give them financial facts that will relate their work to
the bottom line.

Corporate executives have to sacrifice candor on the altar of
company politics. Another advantage for you.

3. Businessowners seldom understand how employees feel,
or may react. Capable of sympathy, yes. Empathy, no.
Reason is that few businessowners have worked in middle
management, administrative, or staff jobs. Most started as
craftsmen or salesmen.

WHAT TO DO:

Instruct your supervisory/administrative people to educate
you as to how employees actually feel, how they react to your
actions. Teach them to teach you. Tell them your weakness for
beautiful, unprofitable equipment, of your emotional quarrel
with unions and government, or of your having gone into
business for some nutty psychological reason, and your present
need to make rational decisions that will keep their jobs alive.
Takes guts.

Corporate executives know how employees feel, but can't
afford to care.

4. Do you give authority commensurate with responsibility?
Employees must often steal both. Encourage them to do so.
Tell your staff it's OK to take authority you haven't given.
That you will fire people for many reasons, but never for
showing initiative. While you instinctively want to hold all the
strings, aren't you always relieved to find someone in the outfit
who will stick his neck out?

Businessowners fight pride. Corporate types fight fear.

5. The Dynastic Urge. To employees, nepotism has three
dimensions. How close is the relative to you? How old is your
anointed one? How capable is he?

If you're concerned that your son, grandson, daughter, or
nephew may drive good employees out of the business,
educate the heirs as to the importance of good help and what
they have to do to hang onto it. If the crown prince can't do
that, forget the dynastic urge and grab the next offer. More

about this is coming. Another example of the impossibility of compartmented thinking in the independently owned business.

Another way you are different is that you must tell yourself frequently that you are not in the people business.

One of the worst fallacies foisted upon businessowners by professors who never met a payroll is that you are in the people business. Have you ever parroted the nauseating sentence, "Our most important product is people?"

It probably didn't occur to the slob who first prompted an empire builder to drool that phrase, that businessowners, under the mistaken impression that corporate hirelings know something they don't, would also pick it up.

Your grandfather hired hands. Now you hire the entire person complete with emotional quirks, and assume responsibility for this pile of psychological garbage. Then you dive into management development and job enrichment. This is the path to financial oblivion via overhead pile-up.

The reason is that you remove specific duties from employees, substitute broad responsibilities, then hire somebody else to perform the duties.

Shifting work down and job enrichment are expressions that conceal the fact that you are hiring two people to do work formerly done by one.

This effort to make intellects out of idiots is based on the unstated assumption that when you need a man to do a job, you can't hire him. Haven't you heard of head-hunters?

Why spend money to teach people to repeat your mistakes?

Sometimes the "people business" idea goes to the extreme, involving an insane reversal in which the owner exhibits unreciprocated loyalty to employees. For example, the business owner who turns down an offer for his company because he is afraid his key men will not survive in a large corporation.

He is right. Eventually it becomes clear even to him that if he doesn't clean out the timeserving deadheads, he will fold.

Rarely is personnel development priced out in the medium-sized company, and practically never in large organizations staffed by nest-featherers.

You are not in the people business, but you are in two other businesses. First in supplying what someone else wants, and second — unless you deal exclusively in cash — you are in the banking business.

If you buy and/or sell on credit, you are paying and/or charging interest. That's the money or banking business.

So when people ask the tiresome consultant question, "what business are you in?" — besides the specific answer of trucking, dentistry, etc., the truthful reply is the money business.

The definitive way you're different is that it's your money in the business.

So don't be ashamed of it or of being selfish. You've earned it. Don't feel self-conscious or guilty.

Part of this book's job is to point out classical traps into which Independent Businessowners fall. The trap we're talking about now is thinking of the money that's in the business as "the company's" money. Businessowners who have incorporated and put some shares in the names of their children are particularly vulnerable to this one.

For some unfathomable reason, many Independent Businessowners lose pride in their success, act ashamed of it, and behave as if they do not own the business.

Such Businessowners — no less than their sons and grandsons — frequently try to make decisions in the manner they think they would if the company were publicly owned. Or, they become so involved in organizational and operational problems they find themselves thinking primarily in terms of profit on sales, rather than return on their investment.

Actually, since not many of you have run public enterprises, your ideas of how their Chief Executives function are likely to be far from the mark. You worked for others before going into business, but at a level pretty far below the top spot.

Falling into this particular trap is partly the result of miseducation from reading articles and books, or attending seminars to improve your management ability. Since the authors and lecturers were addressing themselves to corporate middle-wheels — employees all — you picked up information that can only get in your way.

For example, you may have unwittingly allocated money — your money — to management development programs that may possibly help some supervisory employees get better jobs elsewhere, but will put no dollars in your pocket.

You object to tax money being wasted on public bureaucracies, but at the same time permit employees to deplete your own fortune by building small "management" empires in imitation of the private sector bureaucracies listed on the stock exchange whose return may be less than yours.

Another misuse of your money is on elaborate working conditions. Beyond what is necessary for safety plus whatever efficiency modern attitudes permit, there is no evidence that costly decor, furniture, fixtures, and equipment in offices, or nonfunctional paint jobs do anything for your pocketbook.

Of course, if you knowingly and intentionally want to spend money to satisfy your pride, that's another matter. The mistake is to lay out dollars for uncalled-for working conditions under the delusion that such expenditures are profitable investments.

The worst example, however, is giving in to a superpaternalistic attitude and actually making capital investments in computer or industrial equipment because your employees "want" them.

This is done by almost deliberately not analyzing to destruction the projections they make as justification for the outlay.

Before spending your money, be triply sure you know what you'll get back — and when.

The dollars frozen into your business in all likelihood constitute your largest investment. Don't let anyone influence you to diminish that investment for cosmetic purposes.

When your name is on the door, you don't spend your days either "working" in the ordinary sense, or scheming how to get ahead. Instead, you plan what to do next, supervise the help, juggle dollars, and put out fires.

The way you do these things, and how well you do them,

depends to some degree on your basic outlook. The classical Businessowner's trap is to root your thinking in somebody else's basic point of view. This in turn leads to formation of false premises upon which to plan, supervise, juggle, and douse.

One way Independent Businessowners give up their independent way of thinking — which is the only way they can survive — and acquire a skewed view of their situation, is through association with so-called executives of major corporations.

You rub elbows with them at trade association functions, at Rotary and the Country Club. Your wife and their wives are friendly and your children go to school with theirs. Usually you are all Republicans, work together to support or oppose various political propositions, and serve together on charitable boards, etc.

As a result of all this togetherness, you are in danger of catching some of their attitudes, like a contagious disease. As with leprosy, it happens gradually, the result of continuous exposure. Pretty soon, if not on guard, you start thinking politically instead of in terms of your own money.

These corporation functionaries live in ulcer gulch because, unlike the businessowner, they all report to somebody. They have bosses, like your employees. Sometimes they find it expedient to do the less profitable thing in order to cater to the boss's prejudices, or to help a fellow employee cover a mistake generated by earlier failure to consider consequences.

Your business is strictly to make money, not to build a record which will aid in getting a promotion by showing that you know how to keep things on an even keel without embarassing your superiors.

Remember, your golfing buddy, the Vice President in charge of loose threads down at the ribbon factory, basically can do nothing except spend money. In your case, it's impossible to spend a dime without simultaneously figuring how to get back forty cents.

You report only to yourself, so don't fall into the trap of mentally reporting to somebody who isn't there.

This means that while you can get ideas from employees,

there's nobody to second-guess you. Independent Business-owners must, therefore, decide what to do next on purpose.

Businessowners who decide what to do next by accident, crisis, elimination, personal desires, or compound pique become statistics in the Dun & Bradstreet tabulation of companies that have gone broke because of some vague thing called "mismanagement."

Deciding what to do next is a business decision. So you make it for a business reason. What's a business reason? One that will make you money. Professors of management who have never managed anything more complicated that a complaisant co-ed to the contrary, that's the only reason you're in business.

No use promoting or going out and selling a lot of business if you're losing money on your own floor. First thing to do every morning is list problems in order of amounts of money they are costing you. Then tackling them. Most expensive first. Cash and receivables. Rejects. Customer complaints. Deliveries. Sales Manager sitting and smoking. Chief Engineer complicating existing designs. Office Manager sitting and smoking. That's how to decide what to do next.

Clients sometimes wriggle a little when I stress their basic purpose for being in business, and urge them to square all decisions by the only applicable yardstick—ROI.

They say something like this; they really do:

"I disagree with your attitude that a businessowner is in business only to make a profit and to hell with his employees. Profit is necessary, but I get great pleasure and reward in the knowledge that I'm doing a good job for my employees too, and that as the result of my efforts, upwards of 50 families have a means of livelihood. I take pride in this and I love my work. Why are you against it?"

The answer is that I'm not against it. Nor have I consigned your employees to any particular locality in the hereafter. Nothing wrong with deriving pleasure from providing employment, nor from the knowledge that you are delivering a useful product or service. And it's obvious even to a Ph.D in Economics that you can't run a business profitably unless you enjoy it.

The point is, personal benefits are by-products. If you run the business primarily to gain them, you will go broke. If you operate your business at a profit and, at the same time, succeed in making your employees feel fulfilled, far be it from me to deny you the extra reward of feeling like Lord of the Manor.

Just be sure you are not running the business with that single objective in mind.

Your success will vary inversely with your efforts to run the business in order to get a particular psychological reward.

It is awfully easy to lose sight of your unique role because most business reporting, writing, and lecturing concerns the large, public corporations and the unsupervised supervisory employees who are supposed to run them. That's the second reason this book was written — to balance them off. The first reason was to make money.

# CHAPTER THREE

# When Your Name is on the Note

The fact that it's your money that's in the business sets you apart in various ways.

Public corporations arrange financing, but Independent Businessowners borrow money.

The trap awaiting Independent Businessowners—and strangely enough some bank employees assigned to serve them—is to assume that term loans will be extended indefinitely. Like the huge loans to non-nations called Less Developed Countries.

If public corporations can't pay, the worst that happens is that they are "reorganized." A fancy word giving the creditors shares in the corpse instead of their money. Sometimes a good deal. Or possibly acquired by another company nobody really owns that will use it further to compound and conceal its own errors.

If an Independent Businessowner can't pay, he faces personal ruin, an old-fashioned term.

So when you borrow, be sure that you do so knowingly and intentionally as an individual. Don't think of your business as a "company." Even if you own less than 100 percent, think as sole owner when you hire money.

You may enjoy pretending that your shop has an existence of its own apart from you, the same way a large, publicly held corporation exists apart from the man hired to administer its affairs. They seldom run it. Just don't let the fact that the public and press seldom distinguish between independently and publicly owned enterprises confuse your thinking.

Nor should you be distracted by how you have named your economic child. Whether you call it Ohio Manufacturing Corporation or John Jones Company, it's yours. And as owner, you have nothing in common with hired executives.

That's because if you can't pay, you're broke. Even if you haven't co-signed "the company's" note. Even if the corporate shield — amazingly — actually turns out to protect you. By virtue of your nature as an Independent Businessowner you will accept the responsibility and obligation to pay everyone 100 cents on the dollar. If it takes years.

When a major company goes under, no insider is destroyed financially, socially, and in his self respect. The supervisory employees — so-called "Executives" — just go out and get other jobs. Each can usually establish to the satisfaction of those corporate comedians with Ph.D's in psychology hired by big companies to interview applicants, that his previous employer wouldn't have gone broke if his advice had been followed.

What to do? Two things. First, recognize your situation as an owner. Means acknowledging to yourself that your term loan is not capital, and must be repaid. Not like the long-term debt of a company that employs so many Democrats that the Federal Government will tax you to keep it afloat.

Second, teach your banker your business. He may be only a bank employee, but you can turn him into a banker by treating him as such.

To enable him to convince his superiors to keep your loan, treat him simultaneously as your most important supplier and most important customer.

Never let a banker assume he knows your business because

he is familiar with similar enterprises. If his judgments depend on standard ratios, you're dead. Every show has its make-or-break peculiarities. Do you know yours?

How to teach your banker? Tell him about your business as you would your son if you knew you had only 30 days to live! Then keep him up-to-date.

Personally deliver monthly financial statements. Explain the nitty-gritty transactions behind them. Ask his advice about major decisions. Drag him through your shop every six months. When bad news is in the offing, tell him as soon as you yourself learn about it. A failed customer or supplier. Cancellation of an important order. Possible strike. Cost increases. Tell him before he hears it on the street. The business world is a sorority house.

Have you ever picked up the morning paper and read that a banker shot a client for swamping him with too much information? Has your banker ever told you to stop sending him operating data? Said he had no time to discuss your problem? Refused an appointment?

Coming at it from another angle, supervisory employees of big businesses are hired to manage capital owned by others, while Independent Businessowners own the capital they manage.

Call them Corporate Executives if you wish — the former are still employees. Independent Businessowners are capitalists!

You, the Independent Businessowners of the United States, are one of two groups of capitalists in this country. You are working capitalists. A man occupied exclusively in managing his investments in enterprises he does not run is a speculative capitalist. Takes for his expertise the ability to judge which supervisory employees of various companies will be successful. But he often doesn't find out until too late!

Your survival too depends partly on how shrewdly you judge which supervisory employees will be successful. But you have the advantages of daily observation and of being able to fire the dopes. Passive investors can only sell stock at a loss.

Here is another of those tricky juxtapositions of function

that make it dangerous to attempt to view the owner's job other than as a whole. Beware the expression Management vs. Labor. A trap. Refers, of course, to labor relations, a fancy word for guessing the outcome of the strike-lockout threats which constitute the basis of our economic system.

Newspapers describe these matters as if owners were confronted by employees. Not so. Supervisory employees who receive strike threats, or who threaten lockouts are represented by other employees not union members in the ordinary sense.

Some observers have sarcastically suggested that there is an unofficial union of the high salaried, supervisory employees of the huge corporations that nobody really owns.

The real conflict is Capital vs. Labor. And you are Capital. The people who own big business have no way in which to cope with the strike-lockout threat system except by relying on employees who can't help noticing that when unions get more money that they — the supervisors — automatically get more.

A camaraderie springs up between union officials and management representatives — employees — who meet across the bargaining table.

Such questionable adversary relationships do not occur when capital is represented by its actual owners.

Capitalists devote themselves to increasing the return on their investments. Supervisory employees devote themselves to protecting their political flanks and finding ways to get more after-tax income and tax-free benefits. When you become exclusively concerned with operations you start to think as an employee — a hard-working, dutiful employee! Not as a capitalist.

It's easy to slide into thinking like a hireling — albeit in an overseer capacity — because most of what you read and hear about so-called executive skills refers to supervisory employees, not to owners, or capitalists. Also, most of your friends, customers, and suppliers are employees. Capitalists — who are few to begin with — don't seek each other out to nearly the extent their enemies imagine. That's because your run-of-the-mill owner is instinctively a loner.

At any rate, supervisory employees report to still other, even better paid, employees who ultimately report to Directors. These insufferably self-assured corporate guiding stars themselves are usually supervising employees of still other companies nobody really owns. So the circle is completed. But they don't really have a union. Don't need one.

Your objective is not to impress your boss, but increase the return on your investment. Profitability on a particular order or contract may appear to be excellent, but at the same time delay action financial poison if it requires new, unplanned capital investment.

Passive investors sometimes get locked into securities that go down in market value while continuing to pay dividends. Sacrificing capital for current, taxable income.

It can happen to you. Go into debt for plant and/or equipment to be able to handle a job profitably. Tell yourself you're certain to find other uses for the new investment, and later realize you were kidding yourself.

You are a capitalist, not a marketing manager or production engineer. Don't be a victim of the anti-capitalist propaganda (who could be responsible for it?) that over the years has made Independent Businessowners under forty feel guilty and self-conscious about being capitalists. Made them evade the designation. If you don't identify yourself as a capitalist, others won't be able to follow your example. Then capitalism won't be around any more.

Why this theorizing about attitudes, etc.? You are too busy solving "practical problems" to worry about philosophy?

Very often the reason you often have undefined trouble with questions like whether to buy from this vendor or that, what quantity to purchase, whether to invest in new equipment, and how much to put into an advertising campaign, is that you have too long ignored basic purposes. You are resolving the questions about attitude and purpose without actually saying so, by working on the specifics that should flow from them. Doing things backwards.

With clarity of intent, less time is needed to make practical decisions. Address yourself to the core rather than the periphery of your business.

The more attention paid to analyzing your financial situation and ROI, the fewer ulcers received making operating decisions. They flow from ROI objectives.

Is this mere theorizing? No more than using a road map when driving through strange territory.

While following this road map, bear in mind that Independent Businessowners have been sold money on the basis that they can always pay back cheaper dollars.

The chuck-hole awaiting those who bought term loans was a profit-killing interest rate linked to the prime rate, plus years of working for the bank. Like a prison sentence!

Or did you think that the bank didn't know you would be paying back in cheaper dollars and that you would make it up in higher interest rates? That you were fooling somebody?

"When tough times come, debt is the only thing that can hurt you," said the old-fashioned banker who used some indelicate methods of tutoring me many years ago. Notice he said when, not if.

And he was a fellow who reduced the fancy lingo about money and banking to such gleaming ideas that you should not borrow — no matter how much the bird at the next desk wanted to get a raise by making your loan — without a demonstrable plan for paying back. So he never made President of the bank.

At any rate, now that even campus Keynesians and Washington fortune tellers, a.k.a. White House advisors, are starting to glimpse the truth of the idea that the economy is entering a stall preliminary to a spin, possibly you are drinking cheaper bourbon in order to make bank payments. And you see clearly that my banker was thinking about men who lose their businesses when economic conditions push volume below and costs above the break-even point. Yes, debt can hurt.

But it doesn't have to. Here are some things you can do:

Plan more and work less. Make profit plans for various volumes of business.

Renegotiate your loans whenever interest rates permit you to stretch payments out and scale them down. That's because you should be able to make more than you pay the bank.

Ascertain clearly every month whether you still need each nonproductive employee.

Remember that the outfit that makes money in good times or bad is always and continuously—in good times and bad—on an austerity program.

Write twenty times: "I will never buy a piece of capital equipment unless I can satisfy the worst skeptic that I have a sound plan for making money by doing so."

The trap awaiting Independent Businessowners who continue to borrow now expecting to repeat the process indefinitely is called insolvency. The whole scheme is based on the assumption that you'll always have the cheaper dollars to pay back. Put another way, its' based on the illusion that the business cycle has been suspended.

But if you don't have dollars, you're out of business. That's what the old-fashioned banker meant when he said that when tough times come, the only thing that can hurt you is debt.

Penn Central, Lockheed, Chrysler, and half a dozen banks had Uncle Sam to rescue them with your money. And there will be others. But who will bail out the Independent Businessowner? You stand alone.

What does this mean in terms of day-to-day running your business? It means that the eighties are the decade of the balance sheet. The time to pay down debt and push down receivables.

The mind of every man who is in business for himself teems with ideas, which, when put into execution, are expected to yield tremendous profits. And out of every hundred such brainstorms, one pays off. We forget the others, with their tremendous costs.

Every schoolboy used to know Babe Ruth hit 714 homers, but you have to do some research to learn that the Babe struck out 1330 times. It's the strike-outs that determine your average—in business as in baseball.

This does not mean that your imagination should be put in cold storage. Just its output. Nobody wants to finance wild swings any more.

Apply your innovative effort to lowering the cost of present goods and/or services, and to selling what you have.

Should you think up fresh products to make or departments to start, don't put those ideas into action unless both the financing and payout are short term. Design and plan for the shelf, but hold your wallet tightly.

If interest rates rise or stay so high as to be unprofitable, cut down on volume. Sometimes you make more money by doing less business.

The only exception to concentrating on lowering costs and increasing sales are novel configurations and combinations of motors or meals in order to establish them as new products without price history. That's a bow to the coming wage-price controls.

Reinvestment goes to the balance sheet to reduce obligations, not into long-term development projects which won't pay for themselves—much less pay you—for five years, if then.

Contrary to conventional thinking, the second heaviest burden after development expense is not inventory—which you reduce by not buying—but long term, loyal overhead employees. Supervisory. Professional. Administrative.

Expensive two ways. First, the salaries you've been increasing regularly to "keep up with the parade" while their contribution to your earnings have not. Plus the additional 35 percent of salary for so-called fringe benefits.

Second, the very presence of these old retainers costs you money—and in many cases this is the most important factor—by preventing you from bringing aboard new people with more up-to-date technical training and possibly sharper ideas.

Ascertain what these employees do all day. It's easy to lay off production workers if you simply don't have material ("work") for them to handle. Harder to drop overhead.

Years ago one of the major firms that was still being run by its founder had a man who travelled the company world-wide asking people what they were doing and why. Had a license to ask such questions of anyone in the company regardless of position. His skillful questioning coupled with sharp observation based on detailed knowledge of the business enabled him to relate employment costs to the firm's profitability. He enjoyed great popularity throughout the organization.

This approach should enable you to get the facts regarding your employees. Then ask yourself what would happen if they didn't do those things. Such analyses are offered by consultants for large fees, but there's no reason you can't perform them yourself. You know your business better than anyone else.

So this is the period to protect equity—perhaps the beginning of such an era—in which the strength of your balance sheet will govern the regularity of your meals.

All of which further underlines the impossibility of seeing your business considerations as a collection of textbook chapters. We are talking about money and banking, which quickly become personnel and organizational considerations.

Nor is it strictly an intellectual process—deciding what to do. For when orders go soft, collections hard, and the tax man cometh, the Independent Businessowner hits the austerity trail. And hits it with great feeling.

All requests to purchasing above $9.14 to be OK'd by the top man. No hiring. For any reason. All departments to reduce employees by 10 percent. (Why always 10 percent?)

Egg-timers for long distance calls. Save paper clips. Use reverse side of old correspondence for scratch paper. Chop those expense accounts. Such visceral cost-reduction campaigns can do more harm than good. The insanity sometimes includes amputation of the very advertising that will keep the outfit afloat.

Then one day the sun shines again. Orders and collections pick up. Wednesday golf resumed. The star salesman suggests that if he took Joe McGee and his wife out for steaks, much business would be forthcoming the next day . . . week . . . month. Fine. Tax deductible, isn't it? Don't bother me with details.

And, of course, we should be training people to back up key men.

And so the cycle goes.

A company on a sudden austerity program is one whose owner has been wool-gathering, because the only firms that require stringent programs are those that are not on them all the time, as a regular way of life.

If you're capable of truly accepting the principle, and not just repeating it, that the purpose of your business is to make a profit — an idea that eludes those professors of "management" at state universities and other tax eaters, who assume there's no difference between a government bureau and a business — why shouldn't it be so operated at all times?

Nor is the biggest expense really employment costs. They are merely where it shows up. As an analogy, when water freezes and breaks the pipe, nobody knows it has happened until the thaw. But the thaw did not cause the break.

The primary cause of conditions that inspire sudden financial asceticism is the owner's failure continually to test all disbursements — including wages — for profitability. During good periods.

So instead of installing emergency economics when cash trickles instead of flows, decide in advance how every expenditure — specifically including costs of employees who keep necessary records (not compile data "it would be nice to have"), and promote sales — or investment, will earn a return.

Do this by ascertaining what employees are really doing all day and whether — in the best of times — what they are doing is clearly related to the bottom line. If not, eliminate that function. Now. Don't wait for a crisis. Again, don't think in terms of reducing employees, which is the result. Stop unprofitable operations which are causes.

Lean and muscular men never have to go on reducing diets.

Money and banking are news in these, the eighties. People

who formerly thought that the only interest rates were what they paid on their house, car, or credit card — if they knew — now talk learnedly about prime rates, discount rates, brokers' loans, banker's acceptances, etc.

Polonius advised his son, "Neither a borrower nor a lender be." You, the Businessowner, are both, unless you are doing a strictly cash business. Most businesses — except possibly some retail stores — are lending as well as borrowing.

Your receivables are loans to your customers. Since, unlike a bank, you can't get along just on interest — if you actually can charge it — you have to be constantly re-selling customers on paying their bills. And be ready to cut off accounts whose delinquencies make their business unprofitable.

As long as interest rates are deductible, and the difference can be passed on, businessowners are not sufficiently concerned about high rates. If your competitor pays off his bank first, you are at a price disadvantage. So the cost of dollars is important.

The history of entrepreneurship clearly shows, however, that banks usually have money for customers who have repaid previous loans on time and who present a plan showing how the money will be used to make a profit.

On the other hand, anyone who needs funds to tide him over should do whatever is necessary to sell the inventory on hand or unload any assets not productively employed. No use wasting gas driving to the bank. Not in this decade.

So here are three broad precepts basic to deciding what to do financially.

Don't let anyone panic you into buying inventories you won't be able to sell during the current production or marketing cycle.

Bear down hard on receivables. With interest rates high, customers will try to ride on your money. You can't afford this. Collect. It used to be said that one efficient credit manager could wreck the life work of half a dozen sharp salesmen. This might be the time to let him do it.

In spite of difficulty finding good employees, don't suffer

weak ones. It's tough to replace and teach people, but unproductive employees are like carriers of disease. They infect good employees. Fire the weak ones early and go to the expense of teaching new people unless you can get by with overtime.

There's still more evidence — if any is needed — that a sterile financial outlook can miss what's to be done.

No mama, no papa, no Uncle Sam

We are the orphans of Bataan . . .

If you don't recognize those lines, ask someone who was around in 1942.

Penn Central, Lockheed, and Chrysler all remind us that Independent Businessowners are the orphans of what is left of the private capital system in the USA.

Federal bureaucrats, together with the supervisory employees — corporate bureaucrats — who administer the huge companies that nobody really owns, and big labor are still conspiring to use your money to bail out their own.

This dramatizes the stark loneliness in which the Independent Businessowner functions. If you are going to go broke there is no one to save you. You have only your own wits.

Now perhaps it will become clearer why corporate, union, and government bureaucrats get along so well. Nor is there room for you in their plans.

And is Chrysler the tip of the iceberg? How many other "major" companies will expect ordinary taxpayers to pay their bills as the depression gets rolling?

This tells Independent Businessowners that you accept the leadership, and/or follow the example of no-profit, "Big Business Executives" — whether in politics, economics or so-called "management" — at your peril.

These men cannot, by definition or job description, represent you in dealing with the government, or be on your side in any respect. Directly or through any organizations dominated by big companies.

It's hard to keep in mind that these lads, with their $750

suits, are job-holders with the typical "how about a raise, boss?" employee mentality.

This underlines the need to recognize the central fact of your economic and philosophical isolation. Don't assume there is any lender of last resort as far as you are concerned. If you employ fewer than 500 people, you are not important to any politically powerful group, and if you employ fewer than 5,000 you are still only of marginal interest.

Make keeping what you have your first priority. Getting more is secondary.

Work for the balance sheet, not the P&L. Build the strongest current ratio. Drop unprofitable accounts. Takes discipline. Chop at long-term debt. Don't delude yourself into thinking of it as capital. Don't wait for the banker to call you.

# CHAPTER FOUR

# Arise, Prisoners of Starvation

Don't blame the unions for all your problems, or even those they embody, and/or precipitate. Unions are to a degree an effect rather than a cause — an intermediate step between the source of the problems and the way they show up at your door. That, of course, doesn't stop them from figuring how to get your goat so that you give them more attention than is profitable.

The trap into which Independent Businessowners fall is to develop a non-business motivation to whip the S.O.B's, which is exactly the way a shrewd business agent wants you to feel. There's no gain to him in a relaxed, good-humored Independent Businessowner discharging what he perceives as merely a secondary responsibility.

While in its present form, the labor movement in this country is a fairly recent political invention, tradesmen, craftsmen, and professionals have organized since time immemorial. Big corporations do it too.

Incidentally, according to the AFL/CIO, unions represent only 22% of the labor force.

Other than 78% of the job-holders, about the only people not organized for mutual profitability are Independent Businessowners, probably because they are so individualistic.

Unions respond to the same tremendous economic forces that you do, over which neither they nor you have much control. Their actions are usually misinterpreted by businessmen who think that roosters bring up the sun by crowing.

Roosevelt originally took advantage of economic conditions to create the union voting block. He had foresight, and outwitted both major corporations and Independent Businessowners.

Three additional causes of your union woes are employer stupidity in general, employer generosity (a specific form of stupidity), and people whose livelihoods require tough labor organizations.

Unions simply represent a response to these factors.

Speaking of employer generosity, unions are not very original. Most "demands" were invented by individual employers trying to be nice. These include paid holidays, vacations, pensions, and medical/hospital insurance.

And who were these generous gents who so kindly innovated for the labor movement? You guessed it. Sure as hell not the major corporations, but that former craftsman—now in business for himself—who remembered when Christmas was merely a day off without pay—and who determined that when he was financially able, he would treat "his" men better. Funny how we Independent Businessowners still like to think of ourselves as benevolent slave-holders.

This was not the result of a convention of something like the forerunner of the National Association of Manufacturers or the American Management Association. It just happened as a result of unrelated individual acts by scores of owners around the country.

Later, of course, when the labor movement got under way seriously it was by organizing first the U.S. Congress, which gave it the Wagner Act, then the major industries such as steel, autos, mining, shipping, etc.

Eventually the circle came full round with the organization of smaller firms, many of which presented some problems to the unions because they already — either early on or later in an attempt to forestall organization — had provided their employees with most of the benefits the unions offered.

Two benefits no owner provided of his own accord, however, were layoff protection by seniority and job protection against arbitrary discharge. The labor boys hit these two hard, won elections, and are now using those instruments plus new economic benefits — in their increasingly successful program of organizing government employees at all levels.

As major industry was the labor movement's main market during the thirties and forties, and smaller companies had the honor during the fifties and sixties, government employees moved into focus during and because of the inflation of the seventies and are now ready for the final blitzkrieg. There is no way this can be stopped and that fact is important to Independent Businessowners.

Before going into the why of that last statement, it's relevant to note the misinformation on this subject being fed to cadets in those would-be West Points of the major private bureaucracies listed on the New York Stock Exchange, our correctly-named Schools of Business Administration.

The best way to do this is to quote from a bizarre article in the September-October 1979 *Harvard Business Review*, Holy Writ among the ladder-climbers, bootlickers and back-stabbers of corporate life.

The title of the article is "Are Unions an Anachronism?" The author is Robert Schrank, a "Project Specialist" at the Ford Foundation. About what you would expect from that source.

He believes that the original causes of unionism are ceasing to exist and that unions may be outmoded as "managers schooled in motivation theory and humane ideals of participation replace the owner-bosses of yesterday." He later says, "By educating managers in the techniques of leadership, employee motivation, and effective communication and working morale, the human relations movement created a breed of managers with different attitudes from their predecessors who worked under the iron heel of the old robber barons and their lackeys. Managers do not have the same personal interest in exploiting people that owners did." Later on, "Managers are not likely to turn back into bosses . . ."

You Independent Businessowners will be complimented to have been promoted to the robber baron class. Now this nonsense tells you a number of things. First, the supervisory employees of firms nobody really owns are terrified of, and therefore antagonistic to, entrepreneurs. To them we are villains. That's not important because you're not likely to hire any alumni of Graduate Schools of Business Administration, because they've been taught to administer, not work.

What is important is that, as Mr. Schrank points out, they are "not likely to turn into bosses." Manager in large organizations is a code word for bureaucrat.

Bureaucrats run the government, the big companies, the universities, and if you are lucky, the labor movement. Lucky because by definition bureaucrats are not particularly militant or aggressive. They are defensive.

Only the "lackeys" of an excrescence like the Ford Foundation would identify business owners with the so-called robber barons, whose heirs have created the foundations that provide employment for them.

So-called business executives drift from jobs in large corporations to the government, to universities, and back to banks or industrial giants. Labor leaders move easily from their organizations to the government and back again. Some may have also held interim jobs in colleges and universities.

The final, ultimate joke will be when one man touches all four bases in the course of his career. Don't laugh. The head of the auto workers' union now sits on Chrysler's Board.

Any Businessowner under 45 will see it happen in the good old USA. As Maurice Chevalier said, "I'm glad I'm not young any more."

The significance of all this, as I've said elsewhere in this ramble, is that while Independent Businessowners are the last of the capitalists — the last group to work consciously and deliberately for a return on their own investment — the labor movement is not a danger to them directly or indirectly.

As you can see, with the strike-lockout threat system becoming institutionalized in big industry, big government, and big universities, and with the remaining market for union services being unresisting government bureaucrats who can only benefit if their subordinates' unions get raises, all four corners of the U.S. political-economic circle meld into one big blob of a secretariat.

So calm down, negotiate practical terms with the union if you have one, keeping in mind what the lad or lassie across the table needs to remain secure, and get about the business of selling your wares.

To paraphrase somebody or other, "Late to bed, early to rise, sell all day, and advertise."

And if you don't have a union, avoid the trap of spending more money to remain unorganized than a collective bargaining agreement would cost you.

Also, some large industries have created the suspicion that they agree to expensive settlements to justify raising prices beyond what is necessary to meet them.

The organizations that represent your employees — and they really do represent them, hard as it may be for you to accept the fact — gained their initial position from a little muscle exercised during the 30's, powerfully leveraged by the maintenance-of-membership clauses forced upon business by Roosevelt during World War II. It's as though there were a law requiring twenty million people to buy $25 worth of your product every month.

The stupidity of corporate executives who failed to recognize that they could meet the strong desires of employees for something to say about their work and pay fell right into FDR's trap. This can be done without unions as IBM, Kodak, a few other well-known companies and many Independent Businessowners have demonstrated.

A consequence of this initial stupidity was creation of a new staff specialty — code word for overhead — known as Industrial Relations. Bear in mind it's hard to identify the employer in such entities, just as it is in cities and counties. There is only a hierarchy without authority to enforce discipline.

The Industrial Relations fraternity has proliferated both inside and outside corporations. It consists of company staff men, plus countless individuals whose incomes derive from employer organizations, legal services, arbitrating, consulting, seminaring, writing and publishing. It is a veritable industry. It needs unions the way policemen need criminals, doctors need germs, and keepers need nuts.

Company negotiators have smoothed the union's path to power, thereby making Industrial Relations jobs more important. Each year they "bargain" away authority, and write more complicated agreements.

While the wages and primary benefits agreed to by the giants largely determine what you pay, by developing sound personnel policies and practical relations with union leadership you can control proliferation of runaway authority-to-the-union clauses.

What personnel policies? Those you would institute if your company were unorganized. View your work force as a changing market. IBM and Kodak apparently see their employees as a market for personnel services, and continue to outsell unions.

If customers show a preference for green widgets instead of blue, you do not get angry, demand they take blue under any circumstances and threaten to close the business if they refuse. So use your sales and marketing talents on your employees.

Nor should the owner necessarily handle everything with labor officials.

For example, a client complained that while he formerly was able to work things out with the union President, that fellow had retired and the new man was impossible. His analysis — right to a degree — was that the new president feared his young, militant union membership.

True, the average age of employees — your market for personnel services — is dropping. But are militant, young employees so different from the way less militant, older people were 25 years ago?

The fact that our client owned the business and had a good relationship with the president's predecessor put the new union boss at a disadvantage. He felt insecure and possibly worried — without foundation — that the owner had something on him.

We recommended he assign another man, about the same age, to cultivate the new union official. The two men will be in roughly the same position. Both have to report to somebody. Neither has final authority.

The quality of the agreement this client — and other owners — eventually negotiate will depend heavily on the extent to which the owner thinks in terms of reducing "non-cost item" clauses, which are very expensive, in return for the raise he knows he'll give. Economic forces, again.

Do not respond to the union in terms of beating off an attack on you personally, or on what remains of private capitalism in general.

Scuttle words like "principles" and "management prerogatives," and while taking your ability to operate for granted, negotiate the price you are willing — not able — to pay for labor in your particular business.

In dealing with the union, as in other matters, to the extent you make business decisions for business reasons you'll come out in one piece. And, use will power to restrain yourself from lecturing on free enterprise. You don't really want it for yourself, anyway. You only want it for your competitors. Your business is different. Really needs special protection.

Independent Businessowners who sometimes make decisions based on pride and principle, rather than profit, never do so at greater cost than when dealing with unions.

Even if your business is not unionized, this is important to you because your suppliers and customers have unions. You'll do a better job of buying and selling to the extent you understand the other fellow's situation. And, if it's so important to you to remain unorganized, these comments may help you do so.

To vary the monotony, I'm going to illustrate this by quoting a few actual questions I have been asked, and have answered in my newsletter, *Newsletter for Independent Businessowners (NIB)*.

Q: We employ thirty men in a job shop, have lost an election to a strong union. My superintendent and I bitterly resent this. Union conditions limit his freedom to run things—as you would say, to make business decisions for business reasons. Also, the union pension is twice as expensive as the one we had, and provides no greater benefits. How much should I budget to get rid of this union when the present contract expires?

A: Wrong question if you're going to make business decisions for business reasons. Right question is what engineering and manufacturing improvements to make to offset the higher costs.

Your question is based on the unstated assumption that it will be possible to unload this union either by decertification at a budgetable price, or by walking away from it when the current contract expires.

If the union went to the trouble to organize your plant, they had strong motivation. Such as:

— Some employees were already members, and were holding a gun to the business agent's head.

— Others were sympathetic to the union but did not want you to know it, for fear of reprisal.

— Yours may have been the only unorganized company in the business, and your competitors effectively used you to beat the union over the head, insisting that they couldn't agree to union demands because you were able to undersell them.

— The business agent may believe that the presence of your open shop endangers his chances of reelection.

Pretending to ignore the union after the contract runs out, and operating with a new crew, would be costly and probably dangerous. Nor are new employees attracted to a company that is in an uproar.

If you start a new campaign to dump the union, employees — not to mention supervisors — will be distracted from work, giving all attention to the conflict. This can escalate to the point where people won't speak to each other, much less work together. Sabotage and assault can occur.

The only union more disruptive than one trying to win an election is one that has been decertified. Slapped in the face. Even if you get a majority, those who voted for the union will retaliate against those who did not. A thoroughly no-win situation for the Businessowner.

Even if you win decertification, you can lose again a year later.

What to do? Allocate the funds that you would have applied to a fight with the union to improved product and industrial engineering labor saving devices, and possibly for a psychiatrist to turn the superintendent's head around and get him to recognize that he can do an even better job — though in some ways his wings may be clipped by the union — by improving his technical skills and leadership ability.

And if your superintendent insists that your practical decision is an insult to him, remember it is less costly for him to lose face than for you to lose money.

Q: A recent article in the *Wall Street Journal* said that union membership is declining. Isn't this a good time to fight unionization harder?
A: It is if you want to use your business as an instrument of political change rather than to make money. You might go broke in the process, however, because the unions will fight harder and possibly with violence to remain in business.

Q: After years of having our General Manager handle industrial relations as an extra duty, we hired a full-time man. Too many grievances. He seems to know his stuff, but instead of settling problems, he lets them drag. Is he milking the job?

A: Not likely. He and the union officials are testing each other. Also, while Businessowners want to settle things, unions are politically operated. No urgency. Your man recognizes this.

Union leaders insecure in their jobs have to look busy. Especially if they are new, black, women, or any combination thereof. One way is to find grievances based upon the usual ambiguity of union agreements. Job classifications. Seniority. Subcontracting.

When a situation is settled, the business agent has to find something else to do. Your man is playing the business agent's game. Giving him plenty to talk about. As long as he doesn't settle anything you haven't spent any money. Once settled, the precedent could be expensive. And another grievance will come.

Q: Why do unions fight grievances, when they know their case is weak?
A: The member has been paying dues. He is the union's customer. Union leaders who don't fight for the people who are paying them — right or wrong — give ammunition to opponents in the next election.

Also, some business agents honestly believe that in discharge cases an employer can never be right.

Finally, there is a new breed of lawyer creeping into existence that might be classified as a grievance-chaser. Offers representation to people in lawsuits against their unions as well as against employers.

For example, in 1978, the Associated Press ran the following story from St. Louis: "Some 50 present and former McDonald Douglas Corporation employees have filed a $2 million suit against the firm and their own union, charging 'bad faith, collusion, and conspiracy in arbitration hearings over work rules.' "

Maybe there are too many lawyers. It doesn't take much capital to start a law school, and not a great deal of scholarship to train a reasonably competent soda jerk to pass the bar examination. Perhaps that's why a good ice-cream soda is hard to find.

Q: Our recent labor agreement included more expensive sick leave. Obviously, we have to provide our office and foremen at least as good benefits as the union members. Any reason for not having the two plans identical? Our office manager seems to feel that there's something wrong with that idea.

A: Even an office manager should be able to figure out that it's less expensive to administer one plan than two.

Q: One of my six operations is unionized. The union is driving the superintendent nuts. No matter what he does, there is a big beef. They challenge his every order.

Two employees told me they would like to vote the union out, and asked for help. My labor lawyer advised against it, on the basis that the town in which this branch is located is highly organized, and such a maneuver might involve the entire union movement there, with boycotting and violence. What do you think?

A: I hate to admit it, but your lawyer is right. Decertification efforts are always costly and seldom successful. Chances are those two employees would be harrassed into quitting before the election takes place. Even if you win, which is unlikely, a union will be back in force a year hence.

Your real problem is not the union but the superintendent Engage a consultant to teach him supervisory skills and how to handle grievances, or replace him.

Q: I run a specialty machine shop serving larger manufacturers. We employ about 200 members of the union, and are the largest job shop in the area.

The labor contract has been handled by a citywide employer association which is primarily retail and service oriented. They also represent half a dozen small machine shops which is their only connection with the machinist business agents.

Several larger plants of about 500 men each, organized by machinists or auto workers, have their own industrial relations men. Up to now our association has obtained the same general agreement they negotiated.

There's a complicating factor. The biggest factory here—1,000 employees—is non-union. It stays that way by keeping ahead of the unionized plants with regard to wages, etc.

The peculiar thing is that it is guided by an outside labor consultant who has a regional clientele, instead of by its own industrial relations department. He also negotiates on behalf of other firms with the machinists, auto workers, etc. He knows the manufacturing business, and all the machinist and auto worker officials.

Although his fees are considerably higher than the association, I am considering changing to him if he can get me a better contract, but am concerned whether he might sacrifice us in a strike to keep wages down as a precedent to benefit his larger client, who undoubtedly would be paying him more. What do you think?

A: You are on target when you say, "if he can get a better contract." Your basic axiom is that professional labor negotiators have more in common with their adversaries than with their clients, so bear these characteristics in mind:

Their long-range prosperity depends on maintaining those relationships.

A business agent is a business agent whether he serves labor, the supervisory employees of the giant corporations nobody really owns, or owners. He lives in a special sub-world of power relationships.

Contrary to some opinion, business agents are members of the human race, so they follow the path of least resistance.

There are only two things labor consultants (business agents for management) do: Negotiate contracts and process grievances. Advice on government regulations, routine personal matters, etc., are normally boilerplate.

If the consultant still has his marbles after years in that game, the path of least resistance for him is to continue to have you ride piggyback on the larger companies' contracts.

Unlikely he would encourage a strike in your shop on the theory it would establish an iron pattern for his larger client, because he knows strikes get out of control too easily.

His familiarity with operations is of little value to you. While there is minimum relation between knowledge of shop practice and negotiating a contract, or processing grievances in a formal situation, knowing the adversary is important. But your Association boys also probably know the labor leaders well enough for your purposes.

If you think the consultant can get you a better contract, switch to him. Otherwise stay with the less expensive outfit.

Q: Our Industrial Association is getting ready to negotiate a new union contact. Some of the members think we should demand a strong management prerogative clause. What do you think?
A: Some people eat management prerogatives with mustard, while others prefer pickles.

Q: (From a jobbing machine shop.)
All here agree that a plan must be formulated in case we lose our largest account. Bill and Joe are constantly monitoring the situation and are developing a basic plan.
We are now in the process of rebuilding our work force after a 70 percent turnover during 1977. The union is now a known quantity . . .
We are also in the process of redefining our positions, and drafting job descriptions . . .
A: Guard against use of such expressions as "monitoring a situation," and "developing a basic plan." They can lead to fuzzy thinking. Be sure you know specifically what you are monitoring, what information you are buying and what you intend to do with it. Nor should it take long to "develop a plan" in a small business. A couple of pro forma statements with a list of things to do in order to achieve them will suffice.

Beware the trap of thinking that any union is ever a "known quantity." Unions are political entities operated by political animals who don't think the way you do. You have no way of knowing what events they are reacting to from day to day.

Union politics constitute a full-time career. The trap is almost as fatal as the one a man falls into the day he thinks he understands women.

As to turnover, regard all employees as temporary. The trap here is to think anyone is permanent. Every employee will quit, be fired, die or retire.

Beware of the term "job descriptions." Useless if written as found in manuals of personnel management, where each sentence starts with weasel wording such as, "is responsible for." Just make lists of all the things employees should do all day.

In a slightly different vein, and one which further dramatizes the impossibility of treating labor relations as a "department," separate and apart from the other responsibilities and duties of the Independent Businessowner, a client phoned and asked, "Should we open a branch in a right-to-work state, or move the entire plant?

I investigated and found the plant to be jammed and inefficient. Hemmed in on all sides. Surrounding property owners wouldn't sell for any reasonable price. Poorly negotiated work rules were raising costs intolerably. There were about 250 hourly employees, consisting of machinists and assembly workers. They produced a great variety of models. Many short runs. Customers screaming for delivery.

Here is my report to him, somewhat abbreviated:

"You are enjoying prosperity and the problems deriving from it because government environmental regulations are forcing factories all over the country to buy your products. Their adversity is your prosperity. Never envisioning such volume you've been operating comfortably through a few old-time supervisory and clerical employees who know their jobs and the parts. Manufacturing is based on memory. Profitably so.

"A familiar complication is that the business is owned by two families. At 45, you, the second generation, run the show.

The only remaining active member of the other family is 70 plus. He contributes less each year, but continues to draw a handsome salary.

"You are carrying the entire load. Now that the government has mandated a vastly expanded market you are overburdened, but reluctant to hire a man for some of your duties. Your elderly partner is violently opposed to this. And you too are concerned about the added salary,

"You are handling Sales and Manufacturing while running the business. Something has to give. Your Chief Engineer is no worse than most others. Probably spends no more than 75 percent of his time keeping things in a sufficient state of confusion to make him unfireable. Straighten out production first, then him.

"Obviously you need no financial officer. The fellow who owns the business, whatever else he is doing, handles the money.

"Your accounting and sales records are maintained only for tax and commission purposes, respectively. Nothing for cost or market analyses. Your people in purchasing and shop supervision are OK as long as you are on hand.

"Don't over-invest in right-to-work. The only thing more expensive than a union shop is one that is organized without all the employees being members, with the union constantly pressuring.

"A proposal to move to a right-to-work state is based on the unstated assumption that you would have no union problems after you reach it. Not true. Unions are more militant when fighting for membership than at any other time.

"Unions are winning elections in such states. The AFL/CIO is one of the wealthiest, most powerful lobbies in Washington. A few publicized setbacks do not mean they are finished.

"It takes more than a law to keep employees non-union. A strategic attitude on your part is necessary, plus expensive legal and industrial relation skills. It would be a continuing battle. It is not simply laying out so many dollars and the job is permanently done.

"Moving the entire plant to another city is the greatest risk you could take. It would result in net loss the year done. If not exquisitely planned and carried out, you could go broke.

"The move itself will cost more than you figure. Productivity during the several preceding months will evaporate. Theft and sabotage will be rampant. Secrecy impossible. Customers lost for this reason are hard to regain. They are bitter because they view the supplier as having made a bad decision.

"There will be many more obstacles getting started at the new location than you anticipate. Work-in-process is lost. Finished goods will swell alarmingly in an attempt to take care of customers during the transition. You will go out on a limb financially to buy this inventory. You may have to eat it.

"New orders are excellent now and even if there is a recession, regulatory agencies have built a floor under your business. That's true, but only to the extent that you have a right to extrapolate present government mandated orders into the future. Beward of such assumptions.

WHAT TO DO:
"Retire your partner on half pay since no retirement plan covers him. Hire either an experienced production or sales manager. If your partner won't retire, do it anyway. Swallow his salary. You'll make money on the deal. Adjust to prosperity.

"Before planning a move, first organize inventory and production control so that shipments are made when promised from your present location. Simultaneously a shadow organization may be created for the new location. Compare this to the dual operations that sensible owners operate during the installation of data processing systems.

"A job of this type has to planned down to the smallest details. It's not overly dramatic to compare it to the invasion of Europe during World War II. And once started, everything depends on speed.

"Move assembly department to another location as close to present facility as possible. Lease. Don't buy or build. Real estate will be cheaper a few years out. This is an example of an operating decision based on economic rather than business considerations. Getting a new operation going will be complicated enough!

"Improve employee relations and exercise the rights you have under your union agreement. Few Independent Business-owners do this. Fight some grievances through arbitration. That's less costly than operating two plants separated by hundreds of miles."

It is impossible to talk about the union situation without getting into the murky area of non-union — usually office and supervisory — employees.

Every Independent Businessowner dreams of a snug, little — or big and airy — outfit where everyone works together in egalitarian comradeship, and dreams himself right into the salary trap.

This happens both in firms employing only office people, such as insurance, engineering, or advertising, and enterprises where the shop is organized and the office is not.

One big (or little) happy family, where everyone is paid a salary. Corporate officers, typists, and blueprint machine operators.

But the detestable truth is that employees subject to the Fair Labor Standards Act are in effect required by Federal law to be paid by the hour, because the Act orders you to pay time and a half after forty hours.

When the firm is visited by Wage-Hour auditors, either of their own volition or because an employee or former employee has complained — unbelievable to the head of the happy family! — an expensive struggle takes place to establish who is covered by the Act, and figure the actual hourly rates paid to and hours worked by "salaried" employees previously assumed to have been exempt.

Businesses that pay factory or other "labor" groups by the hour and office help by salary are in the same boat, with one additional reason to put the paper-shufflers on hourly wage: It's easier to reduce their hours when orders shrink and production workers are laid off. Not true that the overhead hours needed remain constant when productive labor is reduced.

What to do? Pay everyone clearly exempt by the hour and

keep accurate records! Nor is there any such thing as a borderline case. If you are in doubt about any employee, treat him as if covered by the Act. Gives you better control and employees know where they stand. Anticipating a question, being paid by the hour won't make anyone less "loyal."

While it is true that years ago salaried employees were not as susceptible to labor organizers as the hourly rated, it was not because of payroll mechanics.

The reason was simply that white collar workers earned more money and enjoyed better benefits than their blue collared compatriots who sometimes had higher skills. For example, secretaries, bookkeepers, draftsmen, and first-line supervisors, by virtue of being on salary, acquired a certain amount of sick leave — conveniently not always spelled out — as well as hospitalization, holidays, and paid vacations, not available to those who got their hands dirty.

Now the situation has been turned around by the unions, and Businessowners frequently find themselves scrambling to "pass on" union gains to the salaried group by pretending they are merit raises, or reaching for reasons to justify not doing so.

Nor does it make sense to anyone who has a higher IQ than an Army mule to say that employees don't join unions for the money. Sure, jobholders want to be treated right, etc., but if they feel underpaid all your beautiful working conditions, and pseudo-psychological monkey business won't stand up against an organizer's promises regardless whether you pay them accurately and lawfully by the hour, or put them on "monthly salary."

To wind up these comments concerning the prisoners of starvation who are being ground under your Gucci heels, consider this client who lost a discharge arbitration and called us in to review personnel and industrial relations policies.

They had disciplined an employee and the union grieved on the basis that the employee did not know anything about the plant rule in question. Turned out that plant rules were made available to employees in a well written, printed policy booklet that had been distributed to all new employees starting 18 months earlier.

Copies were not, however, handed to employees who had been with the company prior to that time. In other words, only about 50 out of a work force of more than 300 received copies of the booklet.

This plant is a subsidiary of a firm listed on the New York Stock Exchange, whose shares frequently appear in the recommended lists of investment letters.

# CHAPTER FIVE

# The Economic Ocean In Which We Swim

Supply equals demand.

Always has and always will. Regardless what politicians say or do.

The only question is at what price.

All the Independent Businessowner has to do in order to know how much to buy, when to buy it, and at what price, is to test the temperature, pressure, chemical balance, and currents of the economic ocean at the depth where he is swimming.

And know what both the bigger and smaller fish like to eat on any given day.

Simple, isn't it?

Temperature, pressure, etc. are translated into as many economic and statistical inferences and indices as you are inclined to look at. After you've mentally recorded all the measurements on a given day, you tell the purchasing agent what to do and pray or cross your toes, depending on your cosmology.

First, since we've been reminding you that the economy — the economic ocean in which we swim — touches all shores impartially, lets look at the international money system, or what's left of it.

One of the most amazing paradoxes of the age is that in an effort to hedge their assets against inflation, Americans have been exchanging dollars for various foreign currencies which are themselves backed by the dollar. Yes, the principal backing — the Central Bank Reserves — of Switzerland, West German, and Japan is the U.S. dollar!

Bear this in mind when somebody is trying to separate you from your hard-earned dollars with stories of the wealth and/or safety to be gained by converting your dollars to francs, marks, or yen.

This is probably a good time to explain why these various currencies are not exchangeable for one another at any determined rate. Why they are "floating," as the expression goes, and what this means to you.

The reason there are no fixed rates is that to have them it is first necessary for all currencies to be convertible into one strong currency, which in turn is convertible into gold.

These conditions no longer exist. Here is the background.

Richard Nixon refused to give gold for dollars — "closed the U.S. gold window" to foreign central banks — on August 15, 1971, thereby shattering the fixed rate system that had been in effect since 1944.

Nixon was not the villain of that piece. The situation had been building for years. He had no choice. Not likely any president could have done differently.

Various countries were demanding gold for their dollars, and if he had given it to them, others would have demanded gold.

To appreciate the importance of that move, review a little history. In the 1921 depression, most of the world's major currencies, except the U.S., were floating. The fixed rate system that existed before World War I had been destroyed by the in-

flation of the war. What really prevented the world from going into a deeper recession was the fact that the dollar was still
convertible to gold. Other currencies were made convertible
into the dollar in 1925.

At that time, the British pound was overpriced, so
foreigners demanded that the Bank of England give them gold
in exchange for their pounds. In 1931, the demand for gold
became so heavy that the Bank of England closed its gold window to foreign central banks. Refused to give up its gold. This
wrecked the international financial structure and precipitated
the great depression, which merged into World War II.

As that war was approaching its end, most countries realized that there had to be fixed currency rates, based on the convertibility of the leading currency of the system into gold.
This, of course, was the U.S. dollar, which served as the foundation for an international agreement on fixed rates that was
made at Bretton Woods, New Hampshire in 1944.

Since World War II, business expansion came about because
of the fixed currency rate system, which allowed for the free
flow of funds among nations.

The existence of a fixed currency rate system is basically a
function of the fiscal and monetary policy of the major reserve
currency country, which, of course, is the United States.

But, as I said a moment ago, the U.S. by ceasing to buy
other currencies for its gold, ended the fixed rate system.
We've had unstable security markets ever since.

You can expect turbulence in the international currency
arena to continue, so the kind of prosperity we had during the
1950's and 1960's is not likely to return until a new fixed rate
system is restored.

What are the likely consequences of this floating rate situation? Depression.

Since the end of the Second World War, you've been told
that we are headed for a terrible depression, but it still is not
here. It's easy to extrapolate from all the data at hand that the
fiscal and monetary policies of the U.S. are taking us toward a
depression, but impossible to predict when it will happen.

The fundamental difference between a recession and a

world-wide depression is its financial dimension. In a recession, events are sales and production oriented. In a depression, the orientation is financial. The basic trouble in a depression is illiquidity and financial distress.

When the post-World War II recovery started, there were some fundamental conditions which militated against the resumption of the depression of the inter-war period.

First, the financial foundation of that period was the liquidity of the banking system. Because of the wipe-out of private debt during the depression and the monetization (means the government printed a bond and sold it) of government debt during the war, the banking system in the forties was in an extremely liquid position. At that time, 85 to 90 percent of bank assets were in government bonds, and 10 to 15 percent were in loans to corporations. Just the opposite now.

The other important condition was the fixed-rate currency system we've been talking about.

The liquidity of the world's banking systems, and particularly that of the United States, was evidenced primarily by the level of interest rates. In 1947, the Treasury Bill rate was 1/4 percent, the discount rate was 1 percent, and long-term government bonds yielded 2 1/4 percent. You know what those rates are now.

In contrast to the liquid conditions of the 1940's, we now have extreme illiquidity, expressed by high interest rates.

Since there are no fixed rates of exchange among currencies of various countries, corporations in different countries can't make contracts.

You've noticed that just as it's impossible to analyze a single operating function of your business without involving damn near the whole job, by the same token you can't observe one characteristic of the financial sea around us as isolated from its other attributes.

The interest rates you pay are intimately entwined with the relationships among the currencies of the world and the trade balances or inbalances of their nations.

Although rates move up and down, since 1966 each advance

in interest rates has been higher than the previous one. Thus, a world depression of greater magnitude than that in the 1930's lies ahead-sometime.

Jimmy Carter once said, "I spent a lot of time studying about the American dollar. Its value in international monetary markets, the cause for the recent deterioration as it relates to other major currencies. I can say with complete assurance that the basic principles of monetary values are not being adequately assessed in the current international market."

Hoover said prosperity was just around the corner and Johnson saw a light at the end of the tunnel.

What is used as currency domestically is determined by law. What is currency internationally, however, is a function of the market. Since no law can be enforced in international markets, the value of any currency is assessed by those who buy and sell, and the market renders its judgment.

There are those who say that the value of a currency is determined by the industrial might, or productive capacity, of a nation. Pretty words. The value of a currency is determined by the liquidity of the Central Bank of the nation which issues it.

The liquidity of the Central Bank, in turn, is a function of the balance of payments of its nation. The U.S. balance of payments has been in deficit every year since 1950, except 1957. And it's the balance of payments that tells the story.

While most economists and financial journalists concentrate on the Gross National Product as a measure of a country's production, the balance of payments figures are more important because they are the measure of the country's competitive position in world markets. Who cares how many TV sets you produce if your competitor undersells you?

Because of our inflation of credit, costs have risen and U.S. goods have lost their competitive posture.

The balance of payments is like the sales volume of a company. When a country is competitive in world markets, it gains foreign currency in gold to add to the foreign reserve assets of its central bank. Thus, gold and foreign exchange assets are to a nation what sales revenues are to a company.

There are three ways in which a nation can defend its currency in the foreign exchange market.

First is to buy dollars with gold. As gold is paid out from the central bank reserve, confidence is restored and the selling of dollars stops.

But U.S. Treasury has shut the gold window. Not likely that the U.S. will defend the dollar through gold sales.

The second way is to sell foreign currency reserve assets. But you have to have them to sell. These, like gold, are acquired from a favorable balance in world trade. And you know how we stand in that respect.

The third and least effective way a currency can be defended is through the interest rate mechanism. By tightening up on credit, and raising rates, the U.S. Treasury and the Federal Reserve could create a dollar shortage which would reverse the skidding position of the dollar in foreign exchange markets. This, however, would not change the lack of fundamental strength of the dollar.

While their fortunes vary with many factors, big companies are now forced, in addition to making calculations in their own area of business expertise, to guess the currency markets. They won't be that good at it. For every winner, there has to be a loser.

This is not as remote from the affairs of the Independent Businessowner as you may think. As major corporations take losses, fail to attract new investment, and can't hire money at profitable rates, employees are laid off and stop buying your products or your customer's products or services.

So in addition to the other indices suggested, keep an eye on the after-tax earnings of the giants. When you take inflation into account, you won't be impressed.

One of the greatest misconceptions is that the government can control the economy, including interest rates, and prevent recessions or depressions. The fact that no government in history has ever been able to do this does not appear to have any effect on office-holders and candidates who promulgate this notion.

The idea that we can spend our way to prosperity first gained popular credence with the introduction of Keynesian philosophy via the Roosevelt administration in the thirties, and those who believed — and still do — that the government controls the economy are the same people who have pithed the dollar by creating ever-greater government deficits.

Then there is the crowd that actually believes the Federal Reserve controls the level of interest rates. Not so. The basic function of the Federal Reserve is to supply reserves to the commercial banking system. It is the liquidity of the banking system which determines interest rates.

While the Fed can supply reserves to the banks, the banks' lending policies — based on the funds available (liquidity) — are what really determine interest rates. Thus rates are simply the barometer of the health of the financial system and the banks of this country, not the prime mover thereof.

To illustrate, a few pages back I compared rates in 1946 with the present. The rise has been brought about by a heavy demand for money in the face of an illiquid banking system and bond market. It was not caused by the Federal Reserve.

There are two basic reasons for rates shooting up. First, the demand for money is slack because of the economic slowdown. Bank deposits shrink, and corporation liquidity, earnings, and cash flow contract. The vast majority of U.S. Corporate balance sheets are extremely illiquid compared to 1960-65. Thus as the economic slow-down continues, rates will move still higher because of reduced economic activity and cash flow

The second important force pushing rates up is the massive deterioration of the U.S. balance of payments which in a sense brings full circle in this matter. In 1976, the U.S. had a negative balance of $9 billion. At the present rate, deficits are headed beyond $50 billion.

This puts the Federal Reserve on the horns of a dilemma. It wants to keep interest rates down to stimulate the economy, and at the same time strengthen the dollar in international markets. As the dollar deteriorates, people around the world sell their dollars.

Since the Federal Reserve will not sell gold, and does not have sufficient reserves to defend the dollar, it has attempted to tighten domestic monetary policy by selling U.S. government securities in an effort to shore up the dollar in international markets. It has not worked.

Thus, you can see the Federal Reserve has practically no control over domestic money rates.

"Bright and Yellow, Hard and Cold
Gold, Gold, Gold, Gold."

Movement in the price of gold is an important barometer for businessmen and investors. Like it or not, gold is the true money of the world. It is the only asset for which there is no corresponding liability. The money in your pockets or on deposit in a bank is your asset, but at the same time these dollars are a liability of the U.S. Government.

Thus, the value and safety of these assets is a function of the integrity of the monetary policy of the Federal Reserve and the U.S. Treasury. Essentially dollars are a form of credit. The base of the credit system is gold and an upward movement in its price is a money market event akin to movement in interest rates.

Gold moves up when trouble develops in the credit system.

The first threat to credit comes from inflation, which erodes purchasing power. The second threat comes during political or financial panic, which threatens the very existence of capital through banking crises, defaults and bankruptcies.

Capital has been moving to gold because of economic uncertainties throughout the world, questions regarding the U.S banking system, and the general fear of worldwide inflation.

Every metal has a supply-demand equation. Gold's equation is unique because it is money. On the supply side, the major sources are South African, then Canadian, U.S. and Australian production. An unknown amount, however, is produced in Russia. Some of the gold the USSR sells has been produced there, and some they buy.

The supply side is easier to measure because of production, but on the demand side the gold equation is different from other metals. One can only measure the potential demand for it by the movement of credit and debt outstanding in the world.

Expressing it another way, you can only infer demand by estimating how much capital that is now in credit will want to move to gold for protection. Significant amounts appear to be in this category.

The principal asset of all the world's central banks—including the Federal Reserve in the U.S.—is gold bullion. Currencies and bank deposits are merely credits issued by governments. While central banks buy and sell currencies, the record shows they buy gold but do not sell it, which establishes the monetary function of the metal. Regardless what politicians say about phasing it out of the system, nations still hold gold as their most valuable asset.

This policy is adhered to even in times of extreme stress, as illustrated by Italy's dire financial condition. That country needed foreign currencies badly for its international trade, but rather than sell gold, its central bank used it as collateral for a loan from Germany. And the Germans were delighted!

The history of the business cycle in the U.S. since 1800 indicates that currency will move to gold when credit is threatened.

Gold, in its basic money function, therefore offers protection in times of stress and strain in the credit structure. Movement in the price of gold from the official level set by the government is a barometer which serves as a long-term warning of impending trouble. The official level is still $42.22.

This is the significance of the rising demand for—and price of—gold. It's not just that a few rich Arabs are buying gold. It is telling the Independent Businessowner that the credit system is cracking.

What to do? Don't let your receivables build up. Better not to have a customer than to carry one to the cemetery.

# CHAPTER SIX

# Bigger Fish in The Sea

Big fish eat little fish, all down the line. As true in the economic ocean in which we swim as it is in the Pacific. The Independent Businessowner who doesn't want to confuse his ability with his ambition sometimes has trouble ascertaining which bigger fish are aggressive and which smaller ones are poisonous.

For instance, have you ever noticed that Businessowners who will not entrust funds to employees, willingly place it in the clammy hands of the employees of the large companies that have no true employers? That's called buying stock.

And owners who won't lend money to people they know well, willingly loan it to strangers. That's called buying bonds.

Who is eating whom in these transactions?

Independent Businessowners who base buying decisons on detailed knowledge and deep study, who seldom accept the recommendation of an employee even if he has two college degrees, often invest blindly outside their businesses.

Businessowners tell each other wisely that doctors and teachers are prime suckers. The truth is that many educators and physicians are successful investors. How can this be?

They are accustomed to studying. A successful member of either profession works harder to keep up with new developments in his field than most of you do in yours. Accordingly, they have less difficulty applying themselves to investments.

While you glance through the *WSJ, Business Week,* and a few trade journals, the brighter teachers and doctors actually absorb hard new material.

Businessowners operate on the unstated assumption that because they are successful in their particular business, they automatically know all about business in general, and extrapolate the delusion to investing. Employees and relatives support this notion.

It always amuses me to see Businessowners trying to find out what is going to happen next in our highly political economy by commencing a program of heavy study of miscellaneous data. Residential and commercial construction, fourteen different measurements of activities in the various securities exchanges, all the so-called leading, lagging, and generally unclassifiable economic indicators.

Some go so far as to study the 100 pages of financial and economic data, 20 stock and bond market tabulations, 15 industrial or trade statistics, and the 50 economic and financial indicators listed each week in *Barron's.*

Three things wrong with this. First, the figures are so general as to have absolutely no meaning to any private investor. Second, and probably this should have been first, the data are largely compiled by government agencies. You know how good their work is. And finally, they are old. Practically anything published along these lines is really a lagging indicator because by the time you get the information it isn't useful.

All you can do is try to judge the direction of the international economy, and its principal barometer, interest rates. By referring to the various influences on interest rates mentioned in the preceding chapter and elsewhere, you'll have some idea of their likely behaviour. To the extent that interest rates hit your customers—such as construction—you'll know how they're apt to influence your profits. On the other hand, your individual business is governed by much more immediate considerations on the part of your customers.

Accordingly, constant study of your own market — questioning of your customers and observing their actions closely — are the most practical ways to make your decisions.

A Businessowner in a specialized industry who would laugh at an individual who proposed going into his field without having first studied, then worked for someone else, thinks nothing of making major investment decisions on the basis of a broker's recommendations, superficial reading of old news, or the tip of a casual acquaintance.

Accordingly, if you already know how much cash you need for emergencies and how to scale your term insurance down as your family grows up, and if you've also done what you can to prepare your estate to pay its taxes, the question how to invest what remains depends on what you want from that investment.

First, look at overall economic and financial environment. As I elucidated at length earlier, we Businessowners are one specie of fish, the big economic and financial world is the sea, and we read economic data to learn abut currents, salinity, temperature, and sharks.

But before that information — interest rates; commodity, stock and bond prices; and international financial and trade conditions — can be intelligently factored into your business or outside investment decisions, your targets have to be clear. That is, you have to decide what to do before trying to figure out how to do it. A good plan for any purpose. Are you after safety, income, or appreciation? Or is your objective simply to shoot crap?

Incomprehensibly, many Businessowners seem unwilling to address the key question of investment objectives, apparently hoping that a magic counselor will appear who will advise how to accumulate vast riches. For some reason, they don't carry over to investment decisions the knowledge of financial reality they apply in business.

If you expect to keep at least some of the loot you earn, it's imperative to think as clearly about your outside investments as you do about the business you own, and in the same way. That is, by making business decisions for business reasons. As I said two paragraphs back, the first question — always — is what to do.

Toughest problem in determining investment objectives is to avoid being swayed by the dominant emotions in this part of life — fear and greed.

An example is making investments "for tax reasons." They take various forms — all of them wrong. Are based on the fact that the investor seldom has a clear picture not only of how much he will save in taxes — which really means how much of the principal he invests and the income he would otherwise have realized on it, he will lose early in the game — against what he might realistically expect to gain down the road. As your grandfather may have told you, you get nothing for nothing.

People who lose at gambling — whether in casinos or "financial department stores" — are not as voluble about these experiences as they are on the rare occasions they win.

Most "tax shelters" are gambles. Nothing wrong with gambling if you fully understand that is what you're doing. Prospecting for oil and other wealth in the earth are popular examples.

The men who sell them are usually on sound ground when they show you all the expenses you can deduct from your income before paying taxes — that's your money, your "investment," mind you — but there's usually much hot air, dreaming, or superstition when they get to the potential big gains to accrue when your well comes in, or the market for your cows, or whatever, is supposed to jump over the moon.

You are bombarded with pitches for all kinds of other investments ranging from conventional securities to inoperative firearms and autos.

Bags of "junk silver." If you buy these, they might really be junk. Supposedly they are dimes, quarters, and half dollars made of silver before the government started to issue potmetal. Are you going to inspect every coin in these sacks?

Diamonds. If you don't know all about diamonds, how do you decide who to believe? And can you get to the wholesale markets? Diamonds are certainly not investments at retail prices.

Antiques. Again, if you know what you are buying.

But all these "investments" are only for money you never expect to need. You can't assume that when you need cash there will be anybody to buy them.

The same rule applies as in your factory, store, or business or professional office. You get nothing for nothing. Even if your name is on the door.

Once goals are determined, hard discipline and self-control are required to stick with them. You might ask, what's wrong with changing objectives? Nothing, if your circumstances change and objectives are reoriented accordingly, rather than by beguiling influences or distractions based on greed or fear.

Here are some rough guidelines:

1. Decide the portion of your savings that is for gambling and how much is for investing.

2. Select the kind of investment that interests you enough to give it regular, hard study. Real estate. Securities. Collectibles.

3. Establish the income/appreciation mix you are after.

4. Study, interview, listen. Treat this program as an additional business that you own, because that is exactly what it is.

5. Invest slowly, commensurate with the knowledge and insights you are acquiring.

At about this point in a discussion of outside investments, clients usually ask about investment counselors. Such counseling seems to be limited to securities, and I've never heard of a counselor who could show that his record over a period of years, encompassing ups and downs in the market, was worthy of his fees. Drop me a line if you run across one.

There are also a few money managers available who will handle your funds on a totally discretionary basis if you have at least two million dollars to turn over to them, and usually don't accept less than five million. They don't always confine their bets to securities. I have reason to suspect that a few of these fellows might be worthy of their hire, if you are in that league.

If you insist on going the counselor route, demand clear evidence of consistent success over at least a ten-year period, and names of clients who will talk to you.

The people he refers you to will, of course, all give favorable responses. Ignore such setups.

Interview these references in person, not on the phone. Engage them in good conversation until they let slip why they are spending their time on you, and possibly reveal the names of other people who have had dealings with the latter-day Baruch you are investigating.

Then check those names. Same kind of interview. Etc. This is what should be meant by the expression, "Investigate before you invest."

Sure, it takes time. Do you want to keep your money?

And what about real estate? Sounds like a free lunch. Depreciation deducted from your income to reduce taxes. Appreciation over the long pull. How do you know it will continue to appreciate?

For some years real estate has been a cinch. You could always sell to a bigger fool.

Many people who boast of how much real estate they "control," who look good on paper now, may well be wiped out when the downturn comes. No bear—or bull—market in anything goes forever.

If you like securities or real estate or old violins, work at them as you do your business. Otherwise you'll be victimized by others who have done their homework. Remember, all fish eat littler fish.

A final thought about real estate—liquidity.

Stock brokers who say that real estate is illiquid, and securities are always marketable, sometimes neglect to mention that stocks and bonds frequently are salable only at a loss. Any investment is liquid any afternoon at the right price. Drop the price low enough and you can get rid of any ill-chosen lot or building as fast as a dog in the stock market — and take just as dramatic a beating.

Summing up outside investments, it's your dough, you've earned it, and nobody cares about it as much as you do. So manage it yourself.

All these considerations apply equally to the financial decisions you make as a Businessowner. Having read this far, you are entitled to ask — and if you've followed me correctly, should be ready to ask — "are there any other kinds of decisions?"

Since most people who own businesses started as self-employed artisans, they think more in terms of their trade than in dollars. Electrical or machine shop practice. Pharmacy. Welding. Mechanical or dress-designing. And so neglect the fact that every action has a dollar sign in front of it. Very irritating if you love your work.

Incidentally, there are a few exceptions to the rule. Women who have taken over businesses from their deceased or disabled husbands, or anyone who has bought a business rather than started it, seem instinctively more inclined to view them commercially than the person who has started from and without much scratch.

This matter of the owner temperament — and temper — weaves in and out of all discussions in this treatise, rather than being covered in the approved textbook manner in a chapter by itself, because it bears on everything you do.

For example, you are using the same brain and accessories thereto when trying to gauge the characteristics of the economic ocean and the other fish, with respect to your business and your outside investments, except that you think less clearly about the latter than the former.

"How's business? How are things with you?"

You and your friends ask each other these and similar questions. Anxiously. What are you trying to find out? Do you really care how things are with the other fellow? Of course not.

You are trying to get a fix on "business conditions,"

whatever that may mean. If the other fellow sells ladies' ready-to-wear, and you make fractional horse power motors, and things are going great — or, for that matter, terrible — with him, you make a wild mental leap in the dark as to what this portends for you.

That's the reason you read the financial section of the papers and news magazines, *Wall Street Journal,* etc. Not that you give a damn for the miscellaneous trivia they publish. But to find some clue that will help you decide how much of what to buy. Which is the basic decision Businessowners dare not delegate. It's only the mechanics of purchasing that's taught at Harvard and other continuation high schools.

And do you really benefit from all this printed matter? Or is it just eye strain?

Police or society reporters who by seniority, senility, or stupidity have been transferred to the financial department, spit words out the way they swallowed them. So many columns by five o'clock.

Independent Businessowners who finish the sports section before their coffee, absentmindedly turn the page to feast their eyes on such effluvia. Before going to work.

Which is one reason so many owners are unnecessarily distracted from their proper, sole function of buying low and selling high. The thinking required to accomplish this otherwise simple set of transactions faces irrelevant word-obstacles placed in its path by newspaper employees who have never even gone broke running a business, but are paid by the inch to tell you what to do with your money.

Don't forget that once the advertising department has done its job, the editorial staff has to fill in the space between the profitable print. So waste no time trying to relate their pseudo-academic lingo to your affairs, nor let such claptrap influence your way of making buying and firing decisions.

The unstated assumptions that pull you off the straight dollar thinking road into this meandering mental bog are first, that the reporters know what they are writing about, and second, that you know what they mean.

Worst thing is, the expressions sound familiar, as if everybody understands the same thing when hearing or reading them. But only a handful of writers—and fewer readers—have nailed them down.

For example, take the learned distinction between liquidity and solvency, so frequently illuminated by unionized, illiquid scribblers to give you financial guidance. Annotated textbooks are published about this. But it's simple.

You're liquid to the extent you can pay everybody off right now. You're solvent if you can pay all bills and debts as they come due.

Here are a few more related expressions that may have contaminated your mush. Liquidity preference. Volumes written. Pages of graphs. Simply means you'd rather hang onto cash than buy inventory, equipment, or shares in companies nobody really owns and maybe not even runs, or lend it out. "Buying bonds" is the euphemism used to conceal the true nature of that last roll of the dice. Frequently is.

Finally, a good one. Liquidity Trap. More learned tomes. Means interest rates get so low that nobody will loan any money. Just piles up in the bank. This happened during the thirties, and—believe it or not—could well happen again. In fact, it could be happening by the time you read this, considering that it takes even longer to get a book published than to do almost anything else.

If you are going to exercise your eyes strenuously and your brain mildly by reading what financial writers write, start by buying a medium-weight, easily handled dictionary of business and economic terms. If the definitions do not seem to correspond to the way in which the terms are used by the author you are perusing, you know you are dealing with a slovenly mind that deserves no further attention. More on this in Chapter IX, and very likely elsewhere.

In the meantime, continue to repeat instructions to employees as they had never heard them before, sell hard, cleanse your brain of sophisticated-sounding syllables lacking precise meaning, and skip directly from sports to funnies.

"But wait a minute" you say. "I want to have some idea about the big picture and what I should know when I am deciding what to do, and as you said, how much to buy."

Like most other things in life, this is not nearly as complicated as the library of books and unending stream of articles on the subject between ads would make it seem.

To anticipate changes and estimate their effects on business and investments we must all make projections. However, most projections are based on recent past, from which you extrapolate at your peril. Take the longer view.

Then follow the *Wall Street Journal* articles that analyze the underlying changes in bank liquidity, and the articles and syndicated columns in other major newspapers on international relations as they apply to political, financial and trade trends; these matters are more relevant to your next six months plans than yesterday's stock market quotes. It would be hard, for example, to find any business not affected, even if only indirectly, by the way negotiations develop concerning Japanese imports — especially steel.

Look for articles that analyze the liquidity of large corporations, changes might indicate the possibility of a major reversal of the trend in force — whatever it may be. Remember, nothing goes in one direction forever.

How to interpret all this data? There are three basic concepts essential to interpretation of events: the international nature of the economy, the business cycle, and the role of credit.

We've mentioned the international economy before. To go a bit further, you must frequently try to get a fix on how badly the politicians of all nations are interfering with, or to what extent they are placing obstacles in the path of commercial and financial transactions.

But it's also important to judge where we are in the business cycle, and, as indicated above, what's going on with respect to credit. Again — and again — what's the direction of interest rates?

In looking for smaller fish to eat, and avoiding bigger ones who would eat you, keep in mind that the economy—the economic ocean—is international in scope. No country is an isolated economic entity. Like epidemics, economic and financial forces don't recognize national borders.

The banking systems, money markets and currencies of all major nations are interrelated. Free international commerce is essential to sustained domestic prosperity. This requires fixed exchange rates based on the convertibility of all currencies into one or two major currencies which in turn are convertible into gold. Disturbances in one area cannot be isolated. They metastasize through the system.

To gain perspective, look back for a moment to 1932. With the election of Roosevelt, the U.S. entered the welfare state via an expanding role of government in the economy. The Keynesian economists promised to smooth out the business cycle and eliminate depression. They assumed a domestic economic framework in which debt did not have to be repaid. Thus, there would be no future business cycles.

A great idea. Unfortunately, man proposes and the business cycle disposes. Rather than smoothing out the curves, the government caused the swings in the business cycle to become more extended up and down. The politician proposes an isolated, planned economy. The international economy, which is still there, laughs. Pity.

The role of credit is based on the often ignored fact that we have a credit rather than a cash economy. Business transactions ranging from the purchase of a tankful of gasoline (the cost of which is largely taxes) to retooling your plant are paid for with borrowed money. The former with a credit card, if such things are still legal by the time you read this, and the latter through a loan. Only by the use of credit or borrowed money is growth possible. Could your business develop without the use of bank money?

A viable credit economy, however, requires periodic economic correction of weaknesses which develop during an expansion. This restores financial liquidity, so that the borrower can meet his obligations and the lender can continue to provide the financing requirements needed. That's the way things are.

In a credit economy like ours, most transactions are conducted with borrowed money. In cash economies like Brazil or Argentina, inflation is the result of printing operations by the government. There are neither long-term lenders nor borrowers.

In Brazil, for example, there are neither life insurance companies nor savings banks. Thus, with the absence of intermediate to long-term capital markets, there is no debtor-creditor relationship. No debt burden hangs over the Brazilian economy. Their government is free to print currency at will. This is how that country's money supply is increased, creating excessive buying power and price increases, and resulting in destructive price inflation.

In the United States, inflation is different. Contrary to what some popular commentators would have you believe, new or inflationary dollars are not initially printed, but come into existence as a result of decisions made by business to borrow.

Each new loan becomes a deposit against which a 15 percent reserve requirement must be held in the banking system. The remaining 85 percent can be turned again into loans and investments. Each new deposit may be multiplied by 6-2/3 times to create inflationary new dollars.

In a credit system such as ours, bank loans and deposits must grow at an exponential rate for a continuation of inflation. Each year an increasing proportion of new dollars must go to service debt.

Therefore, the fountainhead of inflation in our credit economy is the banking system.

In the years ahead, the U.S. economy will very likely go through a series of deep recessions or depressions followed by brief recoveries, as contrasted with the period of growth and stability from 1949 through 1966.

Still answering your question about the big picture—which really means how to hunt and how to escape—the Independent Businessowner will prosper to the extent he makes and follows plans in the light of his understanding of the economy, the business cycle, and the money/credit market.

Just as a street fighter has to unlearn a lot of wrong habits before he can be taught to box, a Businessowner now at the tail end of the Twentieth Century has to cleanse his mind of a number of myths about our very political economy before he can see things clearly.

The impossibility of a single-nation, closed economy, the vigor of the business cycle that Keynes and Roosevelt tried to kill, and the fact that we have a credit rather than a cash economy are examples.

This matter of credit requires further explanation by cleaning some mental underbrush in which many of us are entangled regarding an appendix in our political body called the Federal Reserve.

As I said a moment ago, a basic misconception is that the Federal Reserve or the U.S. Government can print money at will. This was expressed in an article in the May 5, 1976 *New York Times* by Edwin L. Dale, Jr.

"Only one thing is entirely agreed, accepted and understood about the somewhat mysterious and often controversial subject of the government's monetary policy which is conducted by the semi-independent Federal Reserve Board.

"This idea that the Fed . . . can create money out of thin air by writing a check on itself without any deposit to back that check . . . in unlimited amounts. And only it can do so — the Treasury cannot.

"The government's Printing Press is literally in the Bureau of Engraving and Printing, but the true printing press is a . . . man . . . in the Federal Reserve Bank of New York who decides every day, under instructions . . . of the Federal Reserve . . . how much money to create . . . by placing an order in the money market for Treasury bills or other government securities. He pays for them by writing a check on the Federal Reserve Bank of New York. If the order is for $100 million, an additional $100 million in cash suddenly flows into the economy."

This concept of the money creation is nonsense. The Federal Reserve cannot create money out of thin air. Bear in mind that if the government or Fed could control the situation, they would do so, and we'd have continuous prosperity, no recessions, inflations, deflations, or depressions. Obviously, they have not, and therefore cannot do so.

Productive money only comes into the economy when that $100 million in government securities or a portion thereof which has become a reserve in the commercial banking system is sold by the banks to meet the needs for loan demand by business. When borrowers come to the bank, reserves in the form of government notes or bills are sold and the proceeds used to make the loans. The bank then deposits 15 percent of the loan as a reserve requirement back in the Fed.

This, as I said above, makes the commercial banking system of the U.S. in effect a fractional reserve system.

If the borrowing demands of business are sufficiently stronger than the original $100 million, government securities purchased by the Federal Reserve will eventually be multiplied to $666 million in new cash. This is the manner in which new productive money flows into the U.S. economy.

In 1932 the Federal Reserve doubled its holdings of U.S. Government Securities on the liability side of the banking ledger. However, on the earnings and assets side of the banking ledger — (remember, the bank's balance sheet is the opposite of yours — your debt to the bank is their earning asset, like your truck is yours) — loans and deposits continued to contract, introducing severe deflationary forces into the banking system and the economy.

Given the nature of our credit system and the manner in which money is created, deflation is inevitable, but nobody knows when it will happen. That's another reason that if you play it close to the vest, follow a defensive strategy, and work to strengthen your balance sheet, you will be too tough a mouthful for even financially stronger creditors, customers, suppliers, or competitiors to chew, much less swallow.

How to conduct yourself financially in a deflationary period?

Recognize that there is a fundamental difference between a recession and a depression, and therefore between a conservative position in the one set of circumstances as opposed to the other. A recession, which can be confined to one country, merely creates operating problems. It reminds you to cut the costs and improve the marketing schemes that you should have during easier times.

The next depression is another matter. It will be international in scope, leading to a worldwide contraction of credit. To be ready for it, get liquid. Chop inventories. Pay close attention to receivables. Pension funds and other outside investments should have minimum exposure to the stock market. You can't lose on T-bills.

Defensive investments in a recession are not necessarily defensive in a potential depression and money crisis. For example, in normal times or even during recessions, utilities are generally considered safe, conservative investments. The heavy debt load in many utility balance sheets, however, raises questions concerning their viability during a period of depression or deflation.

During a depression, a defensive position is cash and Treasury Bills. But obviously cash has to be accumulated before the depression. Get cash out of inventories and receivables now.

The infrequency of banking and financial crises is such that each new generation believes that those were events of the past. Unfortunately, they are periodic. There were frequent panics in the banking system from the Civil War until the money panic of 1907. That led to forming the Federal Reserve, which was forever to make credit easy and put an end to the banking crises of the past.

What the Federal Reserve system actually did, however, was to create a credit monster which allowed for debt expansion on a scale previously unknown. While the frequency of banking crises was reduced, the magnitude of each was enlarged.

As we move from recession to depression, loan demand will diminish as the better-managed companies repay their debts.

At the same time, weaker firms won't be able to pay. Banks will carry them as long as possible, but eventually there will be bankruptcies — making the depression worse.

In any event, these two opposite forces — one group of borrowers (big fish) paying down loans and others (little fish) unable to pay and going broke — will dry up loan demand, and long-term rates will head down — perhaps to 4 1/2 to 5 percent.

The media periodically tell of efforts on the part of bankers and monetary authorities to defend the dollar.

It is not the dollar, but the international payment system based on currency rates which should be defended. I've mentioned that when Nixon closed the gold window in 1971, he shattered the system of fixed and stable currency rates which had been based on the dollar convertible into gold at $35 per ounce.

Since that time, the currency world has gone from the organized and systematic condition which prevailed with a fixed currency rate system to the chaos of floating currencies — or no system.

This amounts to competitive depreciation of currencies, and there is no mechanism which can defend the dollar or any other currency from violent fluctuation and eventual destructive depreciation.

Thus any plans to defend the dollar are misleading. Defense of the dollar or any other currency is impossible, lacking a fixed rate international currency system and an orthodox domestic monetary policy by the Federal Reserve and the U.S. Government.

As this is being written, the expression "credit crunch" has been moving from private newsletters to the media. What is a credit crunch and how did we get there?

A crunch comes about when the system which supplied credit to borrowers runs out of reserves, and has too many liabilities relative to assets. This is reflected in the level of interest rates.

A credit crunch is usually preceded by skyrocketing interest rates, an inverted yield curve (short-term rates higher than long-term), declining liquidity of major corporations, excessive government borrowing, and banks unloading municipal bonds.

In order to recognize the signals of an impending crunch, bear in mind that interest rates are primarily a marketplace expression of liquidity in the financial system, and only in a minor way are a measure of the cost of money.

For example, in 1948 when the banking system was very liquid with 80 percent of its assets in government bonds and 20 percent in loans, the prime rate was 1.75 percent. In March 1980 when the system had no government bonds of consequence and loans comprised about 95 percent of assets, the prime rate was 20 percent, highest in U.S. history.

Credit demand increased at an exponential rate. Particularly true since World War II, because the discipline of gold on credit creation has been entirely removed from the banking system. Thus, the more credit that is created, the greater the demand. This causes an excessive rise in debt, which in turn forces interest rates up. That's the first warning of a coming credit crunch, and, of course, it has long since occurred.

At a certain point in this debt creation process, short-term rates go above long-term. In the first quarter of 1980, for example, the yield on 90-day T-bills exceeded 30-year bonds. This inverted yield curve — not Carter — announced the arrival of the liquidity squeeze. As it intensifies, it will bring intolerable financial strain into the economy, because the banking system cannot properly invest its funds.

Banks at that time were paying higher interest rates on short-term certificates of deposit than they were getting on long-term loans.

Another step toward a crunch is declining liquidity of corporate balance sheets. The primary trend of loan demand will continue up because so many corporations find their costs rising and cash flow shrinking. They therefore have to go to the bank for money to pay bills, not for money to build more efficient plants. Remember what we said concerning the battle over Japanese imports. We need new steel-making facilities, for example, to compete.

To exacerbate the situation, the government borrows more heavily. It's the same as other borrowers. The more it borrows, the more it has to borrow. Since mid-1979 government activity in the bond market has been accelerating, sopping up credit which would normally go to the corporate bond market.

Once a squeeze develops, it must run its full course until it comes to the crunch. Means that the demand for credit becomes so heavy that banks are forced to liquidate substantial portions of their long-term municipal bond portfolios. Since the banks are the major holders of municipal bonds, this will create a chaotic and depressed municipal market. By the time you read this, we might well have come to this stage of the crunch cycle.

# CHAPTER SEVEN

# Housekeeping for Businessowners

The trap awaiting every decision maker is the ever-present non-business reason for making decisions.

As I once told a meeting of the National Association of Corporate Directors, their principal job is to be sure that the hired hands who run money they don't own, make decisions for business rather than career or company-politics reasons. Since most directors are themselves hired hands, they've never invited me back.

The fact that as Businessowners you are your own directors doesn't excuse you from that same obligation. The only difference is that owners are influenced by a different kind of non-business consideration. Usually it involves—knowingly or unwittingly—treating the business as an unstated extension of themselves, and as a result they fail to see the whole picture.

And please don't boast about your "outside" directors. The first duty of a Board of Directors is to hire the President. If the President, by virtue of ownership, can fire the directors, where is their authority? If you want advice, hire experts.

Leaving aside your original motives for starting or buying the business, or the reason or lack thereof you had for accepting responsibility for a show started by your grandmother, the present predicament lends your privately-owned business an extra value today as a hedge against both inflation and deflation, as a tax shelter, as well as a traditional source of income.

Why? First, because in many cases the liquidation — break-up — value of the outfit will startle you if you find out what it is. Especially if the business owns real estate.

If you're not emotional you might decide to sell the business and just run the property. But do this only if you figure your active years are seriously limited and you have no immediate descendant to take over.

That means analyzing the situation on a business basis, and making a decision for business reasons. More on all of this in Chapters XIV and XV. As you can see, it would be as fatal to organize a book for Businessowners around the idea that any phase of ownership can be studied in isolation from other considerations, as it would be to do a market analysis for a new store location without first finding out whether the bank is interested in flooring more inventory for you at any location, and what rate of interest.

If your analysis shows that from the standpoint of management continuity there is no reason to sell — and there is always a greater demand for than supply of profitable businesses — then you have every right to apply a big factor to the value you place on the business for its importance to your own security. Not to mention the fact that in most cases Businessowners pass on their cost and expense increases to customers more easily than they admit.

Accordingly, one of the early things to do in your business housekeeping is to hire a tax consultant. And bear in mind that many lawyers and accountants who do a satisfactory job preparing tax returns, and even successfully representing clients before the IRS, are either uninterested or unqualified to analyze your total situation with the objective of reducing your tax bill.

The person you want is usually a CPA with a peculiar knack

for ferreting out tax angles that apply to your situation. A puzzle expert. If you don't know a specialist of this kind in your area, write to me and I'll get you a couple of names. You can also use this book as an excuse for bringing in an outsider when your regular tax-preparer or attorney looks hurt and woeful.

What to pay for this service? A flat hourly rate only. Amount varies, depending where you are. Don't be afraid to ask. Important thing is to be sure you are paying a professional fee. Do not—repeat, NOT be guided by anyone who makes such an analysis "free."

Who offers such "free" service? Two groups. Life insurance salesmen and professional fund-raisers for charities. The former are interested only in selling insurance. That's how they make their living. By definition. If their "analysis" does not result in a sale, they have failed. No commission. Some Businessowners may need life insurance, but that's no way to buy it.

Now, as to the eleemosynary outfits. Their job is to persuade you to put a chunk of your dough into a trust from which you will get the income—if any—during the remainder of your time on earth, and they get the principal when you join the acrobats who have preceded you to that entrepreneurial heaven where all deals make money and there are neither taxes, unions, nor regulations.

No reason not to go along with them if you like the charity, and are satisfied with the track record of their investment managers for the past ten years. But don't accept their "analysis" of your affairs. They can only reach one conclusion.

Every month we receive such propositions from hospitals, outfits concerned with domestic and wild animals, civic and fraternal organizations. Sound like they are all written by the same party. Legitimate organizations, run by well-meaning people.

A few questions to ask your Tax Consultant:

Are family members—and sometimes key supervisory employees—drawing optimum current compensation? (This is not the time to worry about paying junior what he is "worth".)

Best type of deferred compensation? Don't let the word "retirement"—sometimes used in company-provided tax shelters—confuse your thinking. Nothing to do with the case. You're interested in moving money from your business into a tax-shelter.

Are family members getting all the perks allowed by law? Finally, are you building the strongest possible case for rentention of undistributed profits?

Remember, in dealing with the tax collector, it's foolish to leave money on the table in hope of avoiding an audit. Nearly impossible to predict likelihood of an audit. Unless you're doing something clearly illegal—which is crazy—an audit is just one more negotiation, or business expense. Nothing to fear if you have competent counsel.

Again, in keeping your business house—let's admit it, we're talking about that no-fun subject called business administration—every Independent Businessowner knows in spite of what he tells his friends, that his chief problems are neither competition, unions, nor even the government.

And knows full well that his most painful torments are the traps he tops out for himself, complete with floor and four sides in administering the business and solving internal problems at cost of losing personal contact with the trade.

Your unique strength is your ability as a single individual to aim the total resources of the business at the customer's pocketbook. You are so closely attuned to the industry you are serving that you sense what they'll want before they realize it themselves. See problems emerging in their operations that can be solved by your ingenuity. True in cosmetics or computers. Transfer pumps or sleeping pills. Nails or noodles.

While the Marketing, R & D, Production, and Finance Departments of the corporate colossi nobody really owns are jockeying for personal advancement and political position, you have already performed all of those synthetically separated functions to get the order, deliver and collect.

The *Wall Street Journal* recently gave the example of one Lewis Salton, Chairman of Salton, Inc., who created an extensive line based on the need to keep food hot at the table. "The business grew, and Mr. Salton added new products as he spied food trends in supermarkets."

A filter manufacturer encountered a hardcrusted maintenance man in the wilds of Oklahoma who showed him some weaknesses in one of his designs which utilized three filtration elements in series. The owner was able to discern a method of replacing the three elements with one, sketched out the general idea on the plane returning home, and in a few weeks had the improved product available. While he was addressing himself to this matter, there was a little distress in several departments because the boss appeared to be preoccupied. He was, and was also years ahead of competition.

An example from the other end of the spectrum — retailing — is that of the drug chain owner who one November noticed that his small inventory of decorative candles was disappearing. A few seasons ago they had been in great demand, but not the past two years. This young man proceeded to make a clean sweep of the candles cluttering up various warehouses in his area, (subsequently resold at great profit) simply because he was able to manage the entire job himself. What if he had had an "organization?"

The Businessowner who works as if he were his own star employee — accounting, tool design, government relations — and sets an example of efficient report reading and movement of folders from in-box to out, is well on his way to depending on his own salesmen — or worse, on outside market researchers — to tell him what's needed next. That is, well on his way to economic oblivion.

Fine to say your job is solving problems, so long as you recognize which problems to solve. Not those in your own shop. You've hired employees for them. Your job is to notice an incipient problem in the customers' operation and move fast with a product or service just as he starts fearfully to recognize the problem himself. You see, if he's any good, he's been out taking care of his customers! If a housewife, of her children. Pretty old-fashioned.

The nature of the administrative trap awaiting the hard-working owner is the notion — frequently the unstated assumption — that he is the only person in the outfit who can handle a particular problem. Especially true if in the area of his personal background. Engineering. Production. Merchandising.

The deeper you get mired in internal problems, the farther you get from customers' problems — mirror images of your opportunities. The deeper you dig in your own backyard the narrower and darker the shaft, and the harder to climb out.

WHAT TO DO:
Get out from behind that desk and go where the customers are. Let it be said that you are the world's worst administrator, but are usually lucky when it comes to "guessing" the market!

But before you go after new business, be sure you are taking care of the business you have.

"Your receiving a check from Bank of America addressed to your business office has nothing to do with us. Once your securities are registered in your name and are in your possession, the dividend checks come directly from them to you . . . Therefore, a letter to the bank from you is in order telling them of the address change."

That was written by the secretary of a stockbroker to a client who, over the years, had effected transactions through him totalling at least $500,000.

Quite apart from her client-be-damned attitude, saying that "having it arrive at your business address has nothing to do with us" emphasizes the secretary's ignorance. There was no way for the bank to obtain the client's business address from any source other than the brokerage firm.

But these are unimportant details. The critical matter is that the firm spends heavily on advertising, and the broker works hard developing new business. Lectures at seminars. Conscientiously studies portfolios and provides clients with detailed analyses of pros and cons of investment decisions. While all that is going on, an untaught secretary is undermining his relationship with a client.

A neighbor of ours has a pool equipped with a time clock that turns the filter pump on and off at pre-set intervals. One day the clock burned out. After a short time, the replacement also burned out. $30 for the clock and $24 for labor each time. The pool owner then called an electrician to ascertain whether there might be an overload. The electrician found nothing wrong and sent a bill for $65. The pool owner wrote to the company that made the clocks.

Somebody at the factory sent back a note that said, "There is nothing wrong with the clocks. Obviously, there is something wrong with your electrical hook-up."

That manufacturer promotes heavily to pool contractors and maintenance firms. Booths and entertainment at shows. Ads in trade journals.

A woman we know invited a burglar alarm firm to quote on a system for her home. The salesman argued that she should have pads under the bedroom carpets that cause an alarm if someone steps on them. She told the salesman that this would be inconvenient, and asked how else the problem could be solved.

"I don't care what you want. I'm here to tell you what you've got to have," was his reply.

The owner of the alarm firm is himself very public relations minded. Active in a service club, Chamber of Commerce, and Boy Scouts. Spends an appropriate amount on advertising.

These business-wrecking actions are not the employee's fault.

In each case, the owner has brought the events down on his own head because he did a poor or incomplete job of teaching employees what to do and how to do it.

Still, when clients ask how to build business, and I answer, "First take care of the business you have," they are often disappointed. Want magic.

Your attention is better invested in repeatedly teaching and reminding employees who meet customers — face to face, on the phone, or in writing—how to keep the account, than in making new calls and improving advertising.

I was a member of the Sales & Marketing Executives Association for many years. A good club.

Their programs, unfortunately, are too often based on the unstated assumption that the sales and marketing functions end with getting the order. The sad truth is that sales and marketing people have as important a job inside their own companies as on the outside.

And if you own the business, regardless who might have the title, you are the VP of Marketing, and/or General Sales Manager.

Your salesmen can be out selling their heads off while inside employees are costing you old customers at twice the rate at which you are acquiring new ones, and you may not know why for a long time.

There is an old saw to the effect that one bad credit manager can wreck the life work of ten good salesmen. More to the point, one poorly or incompletely taught employee can bleed your business to death.

WHAT TO DO?

If you are a retailer, don't stint on using "shopping services."

If you are in a manufacturing or service business, use questionnaires freely, and personally ask customers how they are being treated by your people.

And for all Businessowners: Don't leave teaching and reteaching employees about customer relations to chance. Keep up a regular program!

Independent Businessowners who pride themselves on keeping delivery promises often look for someone to blame when they are late.

The trap awaiting Businessowners who make such promises is that of using the promise as a means of getting the order. Sow the wind and reap the whirlwind.

Not enough margin for error is provided. Takes courage to

quote an honest date, based on leaving room for things to go wrong. And sometimes candor might cost an order. Better to lose an order than a customer, however. If your promises are sound, word will get around.

Delivery promises are based on the following unstated assumptions:

1. That all supplies and materials will arrive on time.
2. That all employees will show up and do the work properly.
3. That all machinery and equipment will work perfectly.
4. That the owner, through will power and magic, and because he knows all about his business, can make things happen.

This is usually the same owner who lectures his purchasing or production staff about the inefficiency of interrupting orderly production in order to get out special jobs, but who, when he occasionally goes out into the field, demonstrates strength of character measurable in kitten-power.

The failure of some or all of these four assumptions to materialize should be factored into all delivery promises, whether for a loaf of bread or a complicated machine.

For some queer reason, supervisory and administrative employees act as if nothing could go wrong. And even the few who have learned to kill people on paper seldom take the next step and blow up machines and equipment—on paper.

In this general connection, one of the most dangerous techniques taught young salesmen is that when a prospect wants to know when something can be delivered, they should ask, "When do you want it?" Possibly a great way to close, but it's an even better way to alienate an account permanently.

The most important tools any salesman has are attached to each side of his head. Called ears.

Met a fellow on a plane to Mexico last year who had sold for a chain of dance studios, for many years. Technique was simple. He said, "Once we found all there was to know about a prospect, we sold her the world."

If you listen to a customer long enough, you'll learn when he really needs your product or service, and be able to fit it into a profitable schedule.

This will enable you to anticipate what customers will buy before the customers realize it themselves.

The only trap here is to confuse your ability with your ambition.

This confusion usually rests on the unstated assumption that labeling the "mission of the business" automatically confers the expertise of the astronaut on the camel-driver. After all, they're both steering a transportation system, aren't they?

Some years ago a consensus grew among professors of business administration and consultants who had never owned a business themselves that there was something mysterious about defining a business. Plagiarizing each other's books and articles, they gradually evolved the "mission of the business" notion.

Thus the astronaut-camel driver comparison. Another version was that if years ago the railroads had understood that they were in the transportation, not the railroad business, they would have gone into airline services. Because they didn't realize their true mission, they went down as railroads.

Of course, the woolheads who evolved this construction had forgotten their own textbooks of U.S. economic history, which consists largely of a series of railroad reorganizations. If the railroads had taken over the airlines, the latter would have been strangled in infancy by the passenger-be-damned attitude of its parent.

In case the weasel word "reorganization" is confusing — as its inventors meant it to be — to anyone under forty-five who has not had his mind polluted by college courses in business and economics — it means a company goes broke — bankrupt — and the creditors get shares of stock engraved on expensive paper instead of their money, and at a fraction of what they were owed. With this low value on new shares, bigger fish buy in.

Another illustration concerned the manufacture of buggy

whips. It was that if buggy whip manufacturers had decided to produce superchargers, or other gadgets to soup up internal combustion engines, their firms would have survived at least until OPEC.

Applied to the burglar alarm business, the concept would mean that it could make money renting guard dogs. The fact that the instrumentation and computer experts who wire your premises may not know a Pekingese from a dustmop is overlooked.

We know a fellow who used to make meters and valves for petroleum products. A consultant sold him the idea that he was in the "measurement and control business." This advice led to a costly lesson in electronics.

If the idea of a mission of the business exists at all, it exists in what you know how to do.

If you know how to run a machine shop and how to sell mechanical devices to the process industries, that's where you belong.

If your expertise lies in selling thousands of items to housewives — supermarkets, variety or drugstores — it does not mean you are in the retail business generally and should automatically consider yourself qualified to make money dealing in furniture, shotguns, or expensive cameras.

WHAT TO DO:

Analyse what you've been doing profitably. On your own floor. Do more of it.

Identify the markets that you have proven you know how to sell into. Sell them more.

Understand that the other fellow's field is not necessarily a broader extension of your own.

No reason to avoid new ventures if that's your inclination, but do so on purpose — not by accident. After due investigation. With a plan to buy the necessary education.

Recognize the special features that delineate your business and circumscribe its rational extention, and the lines that mark other territories.

Cost out the difference. Then decide whether to move.

Making those business decisions for business reasons takes guts. Not just a matter of arithmetic. Anybody can operate a hand calculator.

For example, we're proud of a client who operates a chain of quick-printing shops.

In order to get ahead of competition, he offered to assist customers in laying out their material.

Although the venture increased business, it grew into an awkward and costly situation. The employees hired for this work developed considerable expertise, offering customers practically ad agency work. But they did not fit into the fast printing business, were idle part of the time, etc. The owner—although proud of his composition work—analyzed the situation and decided to eliminate it. Gave up some printing business. Hard to do.

If he refers the art work to the proper people, he might get some printing back.

A candy manufacturer habitually boasted of his ingredients. Eventually he was persuaded to run tests to ascertain whether customers knew the difference between candy made with ingredients of varying degrees of cost. They didn't. He argued with himself, whimpered and cried, but eventually did the inevitable thing rather than raise prices above what competitors were offering in his town.

If you are manufacturing widgets and there's a chance to make the biggest one in the world, don't do it just for the publicity. Make the business decision and build only those you can sell for a profit. You can't get all the business, no matter what line you are in. Let your competitor have his share—the low profit portion.

Service does not mean giving your money away in the form of merchandise or additional work beyond what customers have contracted for. Does not mean doing things free. Does mean giving full measure. Prompt delivery or availability. All necessary information on how to gain greatest benefit from your product or service. And zero-defect goods. All this talk about "human error." Is there any other kind?

But if you do all these things right, don't let it go to your head. Because if it does, you'll have moved in only one generation from shirt sleeves to stuffed shirt.

Then you will be quoting such things as:

"There is no such thing as permanent success."

"Every product and every service has its life cycle."

Those are two of the many cliches of consulting, taught their clients—both big company executives and Independent Businessowners—by promotionally-minded members of my profession.

The bath awaiting the Businessowner who bases decisions on such slogans has about the same depth, temperature, and order of cleanliness as the pond that famous dog fell into when, while crossing a bridge, he noticed another dog with a bigger bone in his mouth, mirrored below.

The constituency for the apotheosis of change for its own sake has escalated to a cult among suppliers of intangible services to business and industry. Its high priests include:

— Professors whose only working experience outside the halls of academe have been summer stints at major corporations where they gathered unsupported data on which to base incomprehensible textbooks to sell to bemused graduate students who knew they were being had, but figured to go along and get it back from the next generation.

— Consultants who create employment for themselves with no economic benefit to their clients by urging on them new products and services founded on hunches only, or irrational acquisitions which create still more consulting work straightening out organizational problems derived from the takeover of a coal mining company by an international travel agency.

— Advertising agencies whose entire revenue flows from innovation because their people are too unimaginative to think of better ways to sell the proven article.

— Business writers and journalists so uninformed that they have to look for something new to write about in order to fill the space between ads in newspapers and magazines.

If, however, based on your personal knowledge of the business — not the type of "market research" that results in the failure of 80 percent of new products — you conceive a new device or department that will clearly benefit the customer — with a one-year pay-out — by all means test the idea.

Nor should everyone whose name is on the door be trapped into what some consultants call "vertical integration" — means buying up your suppliers or customers — with the view of being able to serve themselves plus the customers of the acquired operation.

For example, if you are a manufacturer who has given up hope of obtaining usable castings on time from the local foundry, you might in a moment of madness consider buying the foundry, on the assumption that you can run it better than the lucky fellow who would grab your cash and run.

Even if you can, pouring castings for yourself and outside customers would be like mixing a cocktail 2/3 bourbon and 1/3 gin. Or, you acquire a computer that has more capacity than you need, then try to go into the data processing business. Result: both you and the clients achieve administrative paralysis. Or buy a printing plant for the same purpose, with similar consequences.

Possibly one reason change is so appealing is that salesmen get tired of repeating themselves. Their unstated assumption is that customers remember all the benefits of their product. These salesmen forget that customers have other things to think about, and that competitors are talking to them. They keep inadequate records, do not continually supply new illustrations of successful product applications to reinforce benefits, do not consistently refine sales technique, nor cover and study everyone in customer organizations to remain abreast of true buying motives.

So the easiest thing is to recommend new products.

If you think you need to change to stay in business, bear in mind that aspirin has been aspirin as far back as most of us can remember. Nor have there been that many dramatic developments in drills, apples, tool bits, cream cheese, ordinary office furnishings and equipment, restaurants, hotels, or commercial and consumer timing mechanisms.

WORK AT:

Cost reduction throughout your business.

Sales training, especially for older salesmen who think they know it all but who need refreshers in fundamentals. Hardest thing for them is to sell what you have.

Finding a new advertising agency that will tell your prospects how your products will benefit them, rather than compete with other agencies in the brilliance of their creativity.

And ignore advisors of change who have an ax to grind.

When it comes to administration, some people can't do anything right. For example, I was in a plant recently where an enraged shop steward had torn down the plant rules, but left the company organizational chart alone.

Independent Businessowners who sketch organizational charts for personal use or to instruct supervisory employees, make good use of a profitable tool.

Those who post or publish such creations are posting or publishing a road map to the bankruptcy courts for the crime of strangling their own profits in the name of school-book administration. Looks like good housekeeping, but in reality it is the opposite. Charts scribbled on the back of envelopes or even on nice clean pads help to clarify ideas for yourself and whoever you are talking to, the same way free-hand drawings of new products, or of plant or store layout tell the story.

Neatly drawn boxes representing a formal organizational structure, however, derive from the entity that preceded and inspired the present ridiculous size, shape, and inconceivable complexity of the U.S. Government — the Army. Its civilian pupils, however, have put their military mentors to shame in the art of obfuscating while pretending to clarify.

By definition, no enterprise is more clearly 180 degrees in purpose and procedure from making a profit than winning a war. You don't make money doing things the Army way.

Although the word is popular in the Forces, the concept of efficiency is useless to their purposes — which is to kill enemies. A commander who worried about cost — just the opposite of an owner/manager — would quickly be out of business.

Accordingly, organizational charts are useful to peacetime Generals whose promotions depend on how skillfully they blend all five of the effects recounted above — rigidity, limited function, minimal risk, institutionalized procedures, and politics, politics, politics — lifeblood of military and major corporation management, and death-knell of Independent Business.

Charts grew even more popular with the cancerous growth of government, not just in Washington, but in states, counties (why do we need them?), cities, and probably villages.

Simultaneously they became particularly attractive to the large universities, which, through their most pernicious offshoots — their graduate schools of business administration — supply the government and the huge corporations that nobody really owns with a steady stream of administrators. To replace those who either retire at an early age with fat pensions and anatomy to match, or who ossify at their desks.

WHAT TO DO:
Don't hire trained "administrators," thus imitating the military, the government, and big companies. Their ways are not for you. Use diagrams for your own purposes, but maintain your freedom and flexibility to change direction, alter instructions and rearrange duties fast to meet circumstances.

Don't "communicate" a chart today because your suppliers, customers, and competitors will make sure it's out of date by tomorrow. But your employees will still be protected by it. Such are the hazards of Emerson's "foolish consistency."

"Stay As Sweet As You Are," went the old song. "Don't Let A Thing Ever Change You."

A charming sentiment applied to romance, but the

businessowner who tries to keep his sweet little business at its present size and shape is about to stick his dainty little foot into the painful trap called premature organizational decay.

A great idea to love your work like your wife, but a dangerous delusion to think that in the face of shifting markets and shiftier competitors you can keep it as inviolate as you do her.

A client surveying San Francisco (everybody gets here sooner or later) popped into the office to explain in detail how he and his wife had built a whale of a profitable food service operation now employing 500, and that they're going to keep it that way. No more growth.

His favorite sports now are defenestrating investment bankers who want him to go public and decapitating corporate marriage brokers with backhand Judo chops.

"Stay as sweet as you are . . . don't let a soul rearrange you."

Love may be a more powerful motivator than money, but it doesn't respond to the same song. While your mate may be appreciating, if not totally appreciative, your dollar is depreciating.

But it's your customers and your competitors who determine whether you shrink or grow — you have little say in the matter. If you don't work at increasing your business, your competitor will succeed in decreasing it.

Like the fellow who was producing slide rules but the engineers preferred hand calculators. Or the neighborhood liquor dealer who kept pushing vodka while the gang wanted jug wine.

Or the fellow in the restaurant supply business who has to refuse new accounts in order to take care of those who have been with him for years. He thinks that because he delayed expansion, competition is getting stronger in his area, threatening his long-time customers. Just because I told you that the first step in building your volume is to take care of customers you have, that does not mean you shouldn't thereafter pursue new ones.

Nor are the government and the unions going to overlook you, no matter how inconspicuously you operate. As you may have noticed, they too are busy increasing both your costs and expenses, so you've got to sell more nails, hamburgers, or expansion joints to stay even.

Hire more employees to do it. Therefore another lead man, eventually a foreman or assistant manager. May even have to give in and put on another part-time pencil pusher. All these events change the size and contours of your business, and none of their perpetrators have heard your doleful ditty.

You are not building an organization? Just hire hands? Well, did you ever take a day off? Leave for an hour? Somebody took charge, whether you told him to or not. You inevitably build an organization. They may be good or bad, but inescapably you've hired some heads as well as hands.

Employees who are even a little bit bright require opportunities for advancement even if they have no intention of taking advantage of them, or they quit. And while the rare employee who truly reaches for advancement can be held at the same job for a long period by paying him more, eventually he gets dull and unproductive.

A deliberate ceiling on a business that has opportunities for growth squashes the very employees you need to remain as solvent as you are.

Only the second-raters will remain. Even if a son or daughter is going to take over from you, the second generation seldom has the same command of detail that the founder had, so whoever follows you on a family basis has a still greater need of capable subordinates than you do yourself.

So don't brag about the fact that you turned down offers for your business. Better study them carefully.

WHAT TO DO:
Rather than being governed by "the fell clutch of circumstance," manage your growth on purpose, by plan. Budget your attention to developing not only financial pro for-

mas but the operating steps—hiring men, money and equipment—you'll take to convert pro forma to actual.

And if you're old enough to remember the song, sing it to the object of your affections, not to the source of your income.

Speaking of building business, of the hazards awaiting the Businessowner, none are more extensively scattered beneath the seductive meadows called markets, and harder to escape from, than the land mine of unplanned expansion.

It is a rare Businessowner who has not on one occasion or another sacrificed profits on the altar of expansion by enlarging facilities, opening a branch operation, acquiring equipment, or building his organization without considering consequences and afterwards rationalizing the decision.

This is related to the many manufacturers who insist on a full line because of the mistaken notion that unless they make every size screwdriver they can't sell any size. Nor is it confined to any particular link in the business chain from mine, mill, and factory through distributor, jobber, representative, and retailer. Even true of service businesses.

How to avoid this trap? Simply by figuring out in advance how the new piece of equipment, additional real estate, experimental work, tooling, or staffing will bring in enough additional business to make the venture profitable. By answering the question—coldly and realistically—how much new volume must we have to justify this investment? And then using will power!

Larger firms call this strategic planning, or profit planning. Good words. Again, means figuring consequences in advance.

EXAMPLES:

SAM T. had a successful noontime restaurant in an industrial district. Customers lined up for sandwiches, etc. and did not complain about the delay. Liked his food. So he rented the space next door, put in more tables, and hired another sandwich girl. The result was that although more customers were able to sit down, the increase in total business wasn't enough to cover the additional rent.

If he had determined how many more lunches he'd have to sell to cover his increased costs, and reflected on the fact that he had no competition within a dozen blocks, he would have spared himself the loss.

BILL J. produced specially-designed pumps for the refineries in and around Beaumont. He made trips to other areas in the country where oil refineries were to be found and got some business, but quickly learned that without recognized local representation no real growth was possible. By making diligent inquiry, he found good representatives, orders picked up, and eventually he was doing business nationally. Inevitably, he engaged a field engineer to travel the country and work with them.

To this point, overhead was still under reasonable control. When his field engineer found himself spending a week or two at a time in Southern California, Bill, the owner, decided to move the fellow to that location. Figured that the additional cost — office, etc. — would not exceed travel expense.

Unfortunately, he forgot to consider that while the field engineer was very good at that work, he was totally incapable of generating any serious new business. Also, he continued to travel East when problems arose. The L.A. rep had to be retained, the engineer without close supervision was inefficient — he loved solving complicated, technical problems which did no real good for the company — and still incurred the customary California car expense. The branch office degenerated to the break-even point and was headed below that when the owner terminated the operation.

This owner had expanded into another state, not only lacking correct information on the out-of-pocket costs of the scheme, plus the engineer's inefficiency in the new job, but he also failed to calculate the amount of additional business necessary to make the new office profitable.

JACK W. was doing beautifully operating an automatic screw machine shop, when he conceived the idea that he should do more secondary operations. Several customers had asked him to do so. Like most people of his background, Jack loved machine tools. With this opportunity on his mind, he went to a show and ended up buying a $150,000 milling machine with all the bells and whistles. Sure, it was more than he needed, but it appealed to him. He had, of course, a few jobs for it, but had totally failed to ascertain the sources of new business he would require in order to make his equipment profitable.

He's still paying for it.

## WHAT TO DO:

Make business decisions for business reasons. If I say it often enough, a few of you might start to believe it. Save one soul, etc. Use arithmetic — simple numbers — not words, to guide decisions to part with your hard-earned money.

Let's get back to that full line insanity for a moment. Businessowners who tell themselves that they have to have a full line, have been sold a bill of goods by their otherwise incompetent salesmen.

Nor, as I said a minute ago, is this nonsense limited to manufacturing, although that's where it causes the heaviest losses. We'll cover other businesses in a minute. So stick around, you in retailing, real estate, and services.

Salesmen do it several ways. First, they know how to appeal to the Businessowner's vanity. If they spent half the time studying customers they do trying — often successfully — to psych you out, they would all be rich. So would you.

And they get help. The ad agency is right in there. It can put together a great display showing your automatic resetting, super heterodyne synchronized prune juice homogenizer in fourteen sizes, six pressure ratings, and eleven inlet-outlet configurations available in most colors of the spectrum.

Especially if you haven't come up with any legitimate new developments in the past five years.

If your chief engineer is like most others, the full-line route affords him another opportunity to compound the present alpha-numeric parts and model designation confusion into such a monumental mess that he knows you'll have to postpone firing him for another two years. By that time he can escape with 80 percent of his retirement and join a competitor.

Equally powerful logic flows through the entire organization like hot water in a whirlpool bath. Every department sees its chance to expand as it engulfs them. Purchasing. Personnel. Accounting. Production. And don't forget the outside lawyers and consultants. Big stuff! We'll be up in the majors!

Now salesmen are finding three new prospects a day that will buy as soon as you have a full line. It's never made altogether clear why you can't sell them what you have, particularly since they are buying similar equipment from competitors.

In all this enthusiasm, nobody remembers that you already offer half the line, with 80 percent of your after-tax net coming from a couple of sizes and models, in three configurations at most. All one color — prune juice.

Since you can't get all the business anyway, why not let competition get the part that's not profitable to you?

Retailers fall victim to an analogous intoxication with expansion for its own sake. Or, to create foot-traffic. Otherwise shrewd owners hypnotize themselves on untested, money-losing promotions intended — with no supporting evidence — to induce enough additional customers to walk in and buy all manner of things to make the entire adventure profitable . . . as an afterthought. Foot-traffic is the thing! Goldfish in pharmacies. Delicatessens in department stores.

In a real estate outfit in Southern California that has been successful dealing in homes, salespeople insisted the owner move into commercial and industrial properties. Nobody in the firm was experienced in that field. Results predictable.

An airplane refueling outfit takes a contract to clean the local sports arena, and is itself cleaned out by the Janitor's Union.

Make money in the business you know. Don't play the bigshot and lose it in the other fellow's game!

Nor can you run your business by ritual and cookie cutter. Or, as the administrators of publicly held companies selling below book value say, by policy. A system won't save you.

Now that you've been reading a while, please get on your feet, march into the shop and look at the final line and shipping dock. Is your product buried in so many red, green and purple tags that you can't recognize it? If not, you're one of the country's better managers.

You want to settle things. Every instinct cries out to prevent recurrence when something goes wrong. Whether the error was caused by faulty control, weak employee instruction, or equipment malfunction the urge is to systematize.

What's wrong with this notion?

First, it is strongly endorsed by professors of management and consultants who derive much of their income from installing and writing about systems. Never mind that they don't work!

Second, employees like it because they can hide behind the system. This applies particularly to straw bosses sometimes labeled "professional managers."

They are afraid to use their brains and too lazy to keep a sharp eye on work to be sure it is being done correctly. As a substitute for initiative and thinking, nothing is finer than a new or revised system.

Any system is a list of things to do, expressed in complicated form. The effort to reduce everything to writing is the volcano which spews red tape. You pay for it by the yard.

Most so-called "management" literature recommends red tape, but calls it "standards and procedures."

But it is written for employees, not owners. And some of the employees have big salaries and even bigger titles. You are an owner. Solve immediate problems without creating procedures. Try to teach one or two employees to do the same.

Chances are that each tag you just saw resulted from a product getting out the door months ago that shouldn't have. A knibbeling pin had been left out, a gear put in cattywumpus.

So, to prevent recurrence, an employee striving to emulate your errors inserted an overhead-creating extra inspection point to be sure this particular base was covered and the incident could not recur.

Note, he did not ascertain the frequency of the event, judge the probability of its happening again without this new dollar-eating operation, or figure how many mistakes of this type would have to be made to justify further expense.

Nor did he seek out the true cause and tighten a mechanical or training procedure that would provide a reasonable probability of preventing recurrence without the additional step.

Another reason to pause before insisting on further wheel-spinning is the effect of what has already happened. If it was unusual, everyone involved was sufficiently impressed so that repetition is not likely.

Nor is this limited to manufacturing operations. Happens in offices. Office managers, who ordinarily have some training in accounting, like systems of checks and balances. This leads to nonproductive operations.

So pause and consider before firing a volley of systems into the works. Ask yourself, "Will this really help, or will it just add more overhead?"

Finally, on this matter of Housekeeping for Businessowners, don't despair when things seem to be hopelessly snafued.

All businesses are usually inefficient and ineffective. The only reason they survive is that their competition is usually worse.

# CHAPTER EIGHT

# Free Enterprise for Who?

Many of you assume your battles are being fought for you in Washington by the major corporations that have the resources to do it.

Independent Businessowners who believe this should also believe in the tooth fairy.

The hired help who head the huge corporations that nobody really owns are in partnership with the government people because they themselves are—first and foremost—politicians.

These men are bright, capable, and possess many skills. Real journeymen in corporate finance, marketing, engineering, production. But whose side are they really on?

In order to ascertain to whom a man's allegiance is owed, ask who decides his salary.

The answer, in the case of any jobholder regardless of the size of his company, is his boss and boss's boss. They alone can increase his compensation if pleased with his attitude, personality, and performance, or fire him if displeased.

A hired executive's skills will avail him nothing if he antagonizes his peers or superiors in any personal, political, or

other non-business fashion. You've got to be one of the boys!
Cover all bases. And to female Businessowners who screech at
that expression, one of the reasons women are not going to
crash these inner circles very soon is that they object to the idea
of being one of the girls. But I don't expect many of you to
understand that. Pity.

So the question arises, not only who is a corporation man's
superior today, but who may he be tomorrow? Considering
the frequency with which these fellows switch jobs among major firms, the government, and sometimes universities, we
begin to perceive the mutual dependency that exists among
these enormous, interlocking bureaucracies.

Nor are those who operate the giant labor unions always excluded from the club. The head of the auto workers' union
now sits on Chrysler's Board of Directors. Readers under forty-
five will see men — and, oddly enough, in this case, probably
more women — touch all four corners of the bureaucracy in the
course of a career: corporations, unions, universities and
government.

In a TV ad, IBM made it clear that their principal markets
included education and government. Can IBM's relationship
to Washington be limited to that of a favorite vendor? They
have to be on the government's side.

The media frequently quote private-sector leaders to the effect that "the lack of an energy policy" is responsible for
various national ailments. The unstated assumption is that a
government policy — translate that into more taxes, rules and
regulations — is obviously the answer.

Remember now, it is the voice of the so-called private sector — read large corporations — that yaps about the virtues of
free enterprise while demanding more government policies!

Anyone with even a superficial knowledge of history knows
perfectly well that the essential factor in building this country
into the world's greatest power, with the highest standard of
living for the most people — these things were true a few years
ago — was the absence of government policies.

Sure, major companies routinely fund organzations that

give lip service to personal and economic liberty, but—with a few exceptions—they have to pull their punches. Big business boys are on first name terms with big government boys not simply to gain influence by establishing pleasant personal relationships. They are swilling at the same trough. (An aside to career women—again, you'll get into the game faster when you become one of the girls.)

They are intrinsically—and inevitably—part of what was first identified by Dwight Eisenhower as the military-industrial complex. The size and scope of today's government-corporate-academic-labor machine would have startled Ike.

The administrators of these power centers are devoted to their own welfare—not yours. And it is not in their interest to cause more than ceremonial troubles for their opposite numbers in the other groups.

The March 3, 1978 *WSJ*, commenting on Chrysler's situation, wrote: . . . "a few years back when Senator Muskie stuck Detroit with the current ridiculously high pollution standards . . . General Motors joined forces with the Feds and took out full page ads to sing the praises of catalysts. Why not? GM had the resources, not only to install catalytic converters but also to manufacture them for everyone else. The more expensive and more pointless the government regulations become, the greater advantage GM will have in its relative ability to meet them.

"So the wealthy companies, the GM's and the Exxon's tend to be the most cooperative with the government. Just as wealthy individuals tend to be the most sensitive about such issues as the environment. But everyone gets saddled with the costs . . . "

WHAT TO DO:

Adjust your thinking to the idea that Independent Business-owners have to look out for themselves in Washington and the statehouses. Be sure your trade association is on the job, lobbying and finding ways to minimize the effects of government action on your pocketbook. Phone your association executive frequently, and investigate the degree to which he has become indebted to the Washington lobbyists of the huge, private-sector branches of the government.

Because while you are locked in life and death battle with berserk bureaucracies, you are the targets of high pressure organizations striving to separate you from your money on the theory that the contributions will be used to support free enterprise. Actually you could later discover that you were financing the enemy.

Independent Businessowners who bite this bait without knowing who will get and spend these funds, and on what, pay a high price to feel good by striking an illusory blow for liberty.

You are tempting marks because of your frustration in the face of one government edict after another. We all receive dozens of identical, computerized letters from groups who claim they will save us from the iniquities of Big Government, if we just send money. The only originality they show is in the imaginative ways they spell our names.

These outfits usually list as sponsors many supervisory employees of the huge companies that nobody really owns. Perhaps those fellows figure it's good advertising, or that it will brighten the resumes they are continually updating against the day they will be rightfully fired for having applied their time to pseudo-civic organizations instead of making money for stockholders.

Understand, we are not talking about legitimate trade associations where you know the officers, and probably have been a director yourself. Your trade association—if it hasn't sold out—is the only lobby that represents your business before government bodies.

Nor should you assume that the proliferation and maintenance of bedeviling bureaucracies are strictly the work of government employees and big business. You might be guilty too.

Every time Congress or a state house creates an agency—frequently because a conservative businessman has said, "there ought to be a law . . . "—and people are hired, a non-government constituency is launched which operates to maintain and expand the new entity. This private-sector force becomes that creature's most effective lobby, a fact scrupulously avoided by those who beg for a living in the name of free enterprise.

Look at this, from the April 3, 1978 *Business Week*:

"OSHA's problems are as much political as they are technical.

"For example, the agency is having terrible trouble in making good on Administrator Eula Bingham's promise last spring to clean out the underbrush of 'nit-picking' safety standards.

"Opposition snowballed, largely from the labor movement. And this infuriates the congressmen who keep tabs on OSHA because they thought they had labor's approval. During House-Senate negotiations on OSHA's fiscal 1976 appropriations, Congress agreed to knock out a provision that exempted some small businesses from the agency's regulation if AFL-CIO lobbyists would assent to pruning back minor safety regulations.

"At any rate, labor has picked up a lot of allies: A host of industrial suppliers that have spent money or developed markets based on the threatened regulations are fighting to keep them. The list runs from companies that write standards and provide testing services to outfits that supply color-coded warning signs!"

And many of those outfits are independently owned. Thus do Businessowners become part of a bureaucratic conspiracy that harasses other Businessmen.

There are also law and consulting firms that have appeared in the wake of OSHA, like worms after a heavy rain; who for a substantial fee offer to handle your problems with that and other agencies. Same is true regarding Equal Employment Opportunity and Affirmative Action regulations. These entrepreneurs have a vested interest in the issuance of still more infuriatingly incomprehensible regulations. Like cops and defense attorneys need crime to insure their own livelihoods.

So one Businessowner's free enterprise is another's prison.

WHAT TO DO:

1. Support candidates you have investigated, not vague causes.
2. Don't contribute to campaigns for as yet unidentified candidates.
3. Don't contribute to fancy-sounding committees that claim to be fighting your battles unless you have direct knowledge of them. Usually their only interest in "free enterprise" is for their own benefit. They are real good entrepreneurs.
4. Recognize the true private-sector source of sustenance of bureaucracy, and don't waste energy blaming the government for all woes.
5. Ascertain the strictly business — not doctrinaire — basis for deciding whose side you are on in each case. Truckers or shippers. Airlines or passengers. Etc.
6. Don't hire consultants without first checking with previous clients and finding out what they really did for their fees.

Readers who had previously noticed the divergence in the effect of laws and regulations that benefit the huge corporations that nobody really owns, but grasp the jugular of independent business had their perceptions reinforced by the August 14, 1978 *Business Week* commentary, "The Growing Schism Between Business and Labor."

This editorial describes the now unbridgeable ocean between the publicly held companies in the care of corporate bureaucrats whose highest earned title should be supervisory employee, and Independent Businessowners.

*Business Week* writers Gall (actually his name) and Hoerr say, "Business's single minded zeal in defeating labor's modest attempt to amend federal labor law has sent the two sides hurtling in opposite directions, much to the peril of national interest . . . But, now the first move toward moderation is clearly up to business.

"The proposed amendments to the NLRA would have speeded up the organizing process and provided penalties for employers who violate the law.

"But organized labor has reason to be annoyed . . . The opposition campaign lashed out against 'labor bosses.' " Helpless little guys, aren't they?

"The proposed amendments — even if some provisions go too far — represent a legitimate request for the strengthening of due-process rights for workers in organizing campaigns . . . To labor, business members of (a private group, chaired by former labor secretary Dunlop) . . . reneged on a bargain.

"Labor would support free enterprise and business would support a strong Democratic labor movement." Allegedly said with a straight face. And maybe so.

Leaders of international unions probably are as interested in union democracy as the supervisory employees of large corporations are interested in free enterprise.

Incidentally, the coal miners have a democratic union. Very stabilizing.

As a clincher, *Business Week* refers to " . . . the small-business lobbies and elements within the NAM and the U.S. Chamber of Commerce that led the fight against the labor bill . . . the question now is whether business has let the fight against labor go too far . . .

" . . . even some people in management are concerned that some business groups are pursuing a policy that is too militant. One Labor Relations Vice-President" . . . (fancy title for a functionary who smoothes the transfer of assets from major corporate to union Treasuries — EDB) . . ." for a major corporation worries that the 'Washington Trade Association thinking might prevail' . . . Big Business doesn't want that." Sure as hell not!

Although about 60 percent of the non-government work

force is in shops employing fewer than 500 employees, the AFL-CIO acknowledges that the average size groups sought by the union contains 22 employees.

Hard to believe that *Business Week* would have apologized for Big Business's opposition to the amendments if it did not anticipate the likelihood of major corporations walking away from the "Washington Trade Association thinking." That's your Trade Association.

Employees are employees. Whether they sweep your shop or sit in fancy offices. The more the unions get, the more their supervisors — also employees — get. And they hire good flacks.

Working Trade Associations that help Independent Businessowners make money by influencing government at all levels, sometimes make the mistake of imitating oft-mentioned corporate politicians who call themselves businessmen.

Some things even you have to do are often just the opposite of free enterprise. So what? Don't be ashamed of it. You have to fight on every front to make money. But don't be a hypocrite and prate about free enterprise, because you'll be found out. Unless, of course, there is absolutely no special help you get or want from government.

"Free enterprise" means different things to different people.

Professionals mean using the power of government to keep incompetents out of their fields. They don't believe the free market can do it. Also bans on advertising. And other convenient things.

Moving firms, at least in some areas, get government-imposed minimum prices. Then there was the entire body of "fair trade laws," recently knocked down by the courts. Taxis. Airlines. Trucking. Steel. Television sets. Shoes. None favor free enterprise. All want government enforced minimum prices. Or tariffs that exclude lower cost foreign products.

An article in July 6, 1977 *Wall Street Journal* by John D. Williams explained that, "Important shippers are calling for . . . deregulation of trucking as a means of cutting their freight bills. They include . . . Sears Roebuck, Green Giant Company, and General Mills . . .

"Arrayed against them are some of the strongest lobbying forces in Washington — The American Trucking Association and the Teamster Union . . . "

Some of the same people who insist on mandated minimums for their merchandise contribute to clubs that oppose the minimum wage.

Unions, of course, define free enterprise — they call it free collective bargaining — as the limitless license not only to picket any business, any time, any place, but also to knock anyone on the head who goes through the lines.

The only possible area of general agreement on the term is opposition to new government programs that restrict many unrelated businesses. But here again, one man's freedom is another's manacles. So what? So be sure your trade group is lobbying for and against bills in Congress and state houses, that affect your bank account. Directly. Be sure they are not wasting your dues on political theorizing.

One of the problems here is that self-appointed publicists for private capitalism have for years berated Businessowners for not being professors of economics.

You don't have to take this. For example, Louis Rukeyser of Wall Street Week fame, in one of his columns recounted with horror his discovery that neither schools and colleges — nor businessmen — teach free market economics.

Rukeyser, like other so-called communicators of preconceived ideas whose principal knowledge of Independent Businessowners derive from their own writing, is distressed because we are not theoreticians of the economic system as we would have it be, and that our attention is of necessity concentrated on survival. He says it is our job to "sell" the system by unspecified means — other than making it work.

The unstated assumption on which his little sermon is based is that since Businessowners are the only beneficiaries of private capitalism, they should do "ideological battle" for it. But everyone — including columnists, comedians, and any among them cross-licensed to ply both trades — is rewarded according to his efforts. Even if his efforts are to get government handouts. Businessowners have no greater responsibility to educate the public — young or old — than any other sector of society.

Is there any more reason for you to be members of a national debating team on this matter than it is for English professors to do so?

Rukeyser goes on to say, "The average businessman believes that free enterprise is a marvelous system — in every field but his.

"In his business, you see, there are special conditions . . . (which) are the reasons he needs special protection . . . from Washington . . ."

Is he right?

Maybe Rukeyser — deeply involved with reports and analyses of businesses nobody really owns — noticed that they are staffed by employees who enjoy being regulated and then jumped to the conclusion that Independent Businessowners are similarly inclined. Are they? Are you?

Unless there is absolutely no way in which your business benefits from government action — from import duties to NLRB elections which give you at least some protection against having your employees organized by force — don't you or your Association Executive lecture anybody on free enterprise, and don't send your bucks to Washington lobbyists who claim they will "restore" free enterprise to the land. First, we never had it, and second, they might actually do it. Then where would you be?

Don't let anybody distract you from running your business to make more money. Continue to stimulate others to imitate you. Avoid philosophical debate. Run a tight ship and sell.

Since your attitude is thus of necessity ambivalent toward bureaucracy, don't blame the government for your shortcomings. There are always newspaper and magazine articles describing the piteous condition of companies claiming to be losing money because their resources have been diverted from profitable work to complying with government regulations and executing the associated forms.

Since some of the firms are well known, it's tempting to think that either they or the journalists were kidding.

This sort of thing has even been offered to stockholders of publicly-held concerns by corporate officers as a justifiable cause of poor performance. It is ridiculous for them to complain. They are already filing dozens of reports, so there's no reason they can't take the new requirements in stride. These great "professional managers" have built reputations for getting things done in spite of adversity.

Personnel Managers filling out forms regarding retirement plans and fair employment matters, Engineers designing and reporting on anti-pollution equipment, and Factory Managers changing procedures and writing up their work to comply with OSHA requirements are offered as pathetic examples. As a result, these worthies supposedly are not able to find and teach employees, develop better mousetraps, or improve efficiency. Ain't it awful?

To any objective observer, the employees in question are delighted they have to spend their time conforming with regulations—while stretching and milking the job at that—because it provides a magnificent excuse for not doing any real work and thereby being held responsible for projects that don't turn out well.

The "Managers" who feel paralyzed because of new regulations are not businessmen, but merely highly paid employees with typical employee outlooks. They have discovered a great reason to do nothing while hiding behind the Government demands. What can you expect? If they had any real stake in the business, they would work nights instead of crying like little kids.

Government agencies always spin off people into private industry. This is most conspicuous in the old-line regulatory bodies. Men who have spent half their lives in Washington later turn up as employees of companies in the industries they formerly regulated. Certain self-appointed guardians of public morality profess to see something sinister in this, but it's really quite logical. Experienced bureaucrats alone know how to comply with the requirements they previously promulgated.

Accordingly, the businesslike move is to hire a person with suitable background in a government technical department, such as one involved with pollution or safety. Pension and fair employment follow closely. An engineer who can deal with pollution regulations forms can learn to cope with those concerning safety and personnel. It may not work as readily the other way.

Their salaries are a legitimate element of cost. Whether you are a manufacturer, distributor, or retailer, the customer has to pay for all this regardless who does the work. It's the same whether you use regular employees and thus lose their alleged contribution to profitability or hire a government relations man. Or woman, if you can find one. Affirmatively.

Keeping overhead down is a proper objective. This sort of activity, however, is actually a form of production work forced upon you by the government, and does not constitute overhead created by your business. The fact that you may not find it economically justifiable is besides the point. Nor is how you handle it from an accounting standpoint material.

If you're worried that your costs will get too high, remember that your competitors are in the same boat. They too will have to raise prices to cover the costs of compliance or go broke.

To ignore a government request can lead to more expense in negotiations and possible penalties than would be incurred by trying to respond. Besides, you don't need to be over-zealous. Do the best you can. Washington and the state capitals expect mistakes and will work with you to correct them. Use the experience gained in other types of government reporting.

We've always had government forms. Social Security, Unemployment Insurance, Internal Revenue, State and Municipal tax collecting agencies, plus others that apply to specific industries.

If you were around during World War II, the Korean shoot-out, or Nixon's "peacetime" wage-price controls, you remember the reports concerning material, wages, prices, etc.

Now you have more, because additional government agencies have been created. And that's only the beginning. Don't panic and don't waste energy on righteous indignation. If you want to fight the government, don't use your business as a weapon. You will lose. The only way to reduce government controls is to elect different people to Congress. Traditionally Businessowners are not politicians. So make business decisions for business reasons, not to work off steam.

This will get harder as the U.S. moves toward a war economy — which power-mad politicians will create with or without actual conflict. In its early stages, the principal unstated assumption that delivers Independent Businessowners to the bankruptcy courts is that they have a right to exist.

And politicians love it. Not war, but the war economy, which by definition increases their power and mutes criticism.

What are the characteristics of a war economy?
— Allocations of employees and materials by the government.
— Wage and price controls.
— Narrowing of personal liberty, and constant snooping by government spies. 1984 no longer a satire, but the real thing.

Businessowners who propose to survive this period know better than simply to "adjust" to the new circumstances. To use a revolting expression, "affirmative action" is necessary.

WHAT TO DO:
1. Recognize that as a Businessowner, you are in a stronger position for ultimate financial survival than any employee — even the head of a large, private bureaucracy listed on the stock exchange.

Because you can acquire assets and write them off with pre-tax dollars. Assets you will use to advantage later. The government may even finance the deals. Besides, you can't get fired or reassigned to another job by the government.
2. Make a definite, clear statement to yourself that you are in

a period of economic and possibly personal regimentation, that you are not going to waste energy — and possibly risk imprisonment — by fighting it, and that you are going to make some money come hell or high water. Legally.

3.   Decide why you have a right to exist in a war economy. What does your business do for the "war effort?" You don't actually have to be making machine guns, or even supplies for a machine gun factory.

Think imaginatively in terms of the "war worker." This critter has to be properly served in all respects. Fed. Clothed. Pilled. Housed. Transported. Awakened. Amused. (Morale is important.)

4.   Write that decision in detail. You're going to use it as the first paragraph of countless letters covering forms filled out for a variety and quantity of government offices beyond the combined, fevered dreams of a dozen of today's bureaucrats breathing pure opium.

Nor should you let price of authorship prevent you from improving and updating this virtual constitution for your business. With experience, you'll learn amazing things about your own show and its overarching role in our national destiny.

And let your employees contribute to the bill of particulars. People who heretofore appeared dull, stodgy, and without an idea in their heads will become shrewdly creative when the notion permeates their skulls they might be drafted into the Infantry or a coal mine lacking environmental or other amenities.

5.   Re-read Paragraph 3. Where you are not involved with production or transportation of goods, or the rendering of services, that have a reasonable relationship to military activity or employees of firms directly in such work, get involved.

In plain English, start now to sell your services to factories, hospitals, and the everyday suppliers to them. If you are in manufacturing, go after both direct and subcontracting. Start to build these bridges this minute! And don't let the need for an Affirmative Action plan stop you. It's all money. Just pencil it out, and add the cost to your price.

In warning you that in the early stages of a war economy your most dangerous unstated assumption is that you have a right to exist, I was not referring to complying with more regulations and filling out additional impossible forms. Those things are merely expenses.

The problem will be getting permission to hire employees and buy materials.

A parallel mistaken assumption is that all the same principles that govern business decisions in the absence of a war economy continue to operate when it comes.

For example, what do you consider overhead? All successful businessowners learn to fight overhead buildup. As I mentioned briefly earlier, in a war economy, record keeping that would otherwise be overhead becomes direct cost.

The important documents relate to purchasing and personnel. Addressing this issue to purchasing, normally you only keep records that are useful in making buying decisions. Now you must also keep records that will do two other things required by the war-preparation environment.

—  Justify to one or more government agencies the factoring of cost increases into your prices.
—  Establish to still other bureaus—and don't assume there will be only one such board—your right to buy goods or materials.

Both additional histories are necessary if you're going to have a business to run between now and the time a new balance of power is struck between the United States and Russia—unless actual war comes first.

If a computer is handling purchasing and inventory control, don't spend money reprogramming at this time. That might be practical when the next overlay of bureaucracy is settled in, but for the present you'll be money ahead to do the extra work manually.

You need quick reference to all sources, both by supplier and type of goods or commodities. Show quantities, prices, lead time quoted, shipping promises made, actual shipping dates, and quality control reports for each shipment. Cross-reference supplier and goods records.

It may be more of a nuisance than it's worth for your ac-countant to make a direct charge against cost of production, if you're only talking about one or two extra people. The impor-tant thing is that you recognize these costs as of a truly necessary and direct nature. Reducing them is false economy.

The foregoing does not apply exclusively to manufacturers. The same type of information is necessary for jobbers, distributors, and retailers who will have to get bureaucratic OK to continue to buy goods and serve customers.

This paper work will back up reports and requests to government for allocations of materials, supplies, and goods.

Even Carter, in one of his otherwise incomprehensible speeches recognized that coping with increasing regulations has created a new profession. Lawyers and CPA's are swamped and unless they have staff specializing in these mat-ters, are not much better off than businessowners.

Most of the consultants who will be springing up, offering to represent you in these matters, will have less expertise than you yourself.

Now on the personnel side, although you know that most personnel work is baloney, a good deal of it will be necessary if you are to be permitted by the government to have any employees as the war economy heats up.

The complicated, redundant records, out of date job descriptions, etc., that characterize the paraphernalia that personnel department employees continue to smear around on their table seldom if ever put any money in the owner's bank account.

Again, the cost of the clerical load is mitigated only by the fact that your competitors will have to do the same thing. Get the jump on them early.

I've referred to preparing for priorities, allocations, or what have you regarding materials.

The same kind of record keeping which in the purchasing function is now a legitimate direct cost — not overhead — also applies to personnel records.

If you haven't already done so, sit right down and dictate job descriptions for every function in your company, and group them together into half a dozen or so wage levels. Establish wage-rate ranges for those levels and create a personnel record for each employee showing when he moved from one to the other and when there was a change of rate in accordance with a change in job classification held.

Do this in a manner that enables you to go back and pick it up for the past couple of years.

You have to build a record. And the nutty thing is that you, the owner, will be straining at the leash to increase rather than hold wages and salaries down. You'll do this in order to get employees.

These records are to establish the fact that you've been following that system of so-called personnel administration for a long time. The further back these documents go before the base year, the more credible they will be to the bureaucrats who will be governing your employment practices.

This is because the media, most of the people, and some of the businessowners too, are unable or unwilling to recognize that true nature of what politicians are talking about when they use the word "draft."

It is not the same military-only conscription used in World War I, World War II, the Korean and Vietnam wars. If you pay close attention to the lingo flying around among congressional staffers, miscellaneous time servers in the Executive branch of the Federal Government, and reporters, you'll notice a peculiar interchange between the word "draft" and the expression "National Service."

The purpose is to finesse the proposition in order to include women without making it appear that they will be subject to front line duty.

The reason for this reticence is a mystery since the ferocity of women fighters is so great that the Israelis pulled them out of the front lines. Showed no mercy. Didn't know when to stop. Also it's well known in our own country that women can shoot straight.

The point is that the "draft"—which will evolve into National Service, really means not merely pulling people into the armed forces, but giving the politicians authority to decide who works where. Call it Communism, Facism, Socialism, National Socialism, Totalitarianism or just plain Tyranny—the result is the same.

The country is headed in this direction and although we may not go the full distance, Businessowners who want to have a business to run, sell, bequeath, or even liquidate during the next five years, would be well advised to make the preparations indicated.

If you have teenagers at home, then encourage them to learn trades. Carpenter. Electrician. Machinist. Repairman. The colleges and universities, subsidized since World War II either by the GI Bill or by the parents of boys avoiding military service, are about to experience a private little depression of their own.

Before going after government contracts, recognize that you will be in line to be caught in a nutcracker and then hit with a hammer. And as I said a while ago, pencil it out and price it right.

One arm of the nutcracker is the Office of Federal Contract Compliance Programs (OFCCP), and the other is wage-price controls.

The hammer blow will come from the regulations that will derive from whatever form the national service (draft) law takes. It will be impossible to comply with all regulations simultaneously.

And if you don't seek government contracts, better look again. You'll be amazed when the bureaucracy classified you as the equivalent of government contractors for the purposes of OFCCP, or hits you under Equal Employment Opportunity Commission (EEOC) regulations. More on this later.

Back to square one.

Executive Order No. 11246, issued by Lyndon Johnson in 1965, requires employers who contract with the Federal government to install a written Affirmative Action Program (AAP).

Enforcement has only now been assigned to the OFCCP. Except for such well publicized cases as the multi-million dollar judgement against ATT (more on this and why it concerns you below), old 11246 has been a sleeping rattlesnake.

But the air is getting chilly, and this little charmer is wiggling. It can strike in any direction.

Compliance with 11246 begins at the bid stage. Every bidder must state it has an AAP, or be ineligible for award.

Don't let previous lax enforcement lull you into a false sense of security. If you're doing business with the Federal government, and don't have an AAP, get moving. The OFCCP is gearing up to enforce regulations with a vengeance.

Sure, they are starting with the larger firms, but will get to you eventually.

Until late in 1978 OFCCP had delegated its enforcement power to 16 other Federal agencies, such as the Departments of Energy, Defense, Interior, etc., with instructions to attack on an industry-by-industry basis.

On October 1, 1978, the Department of Labor began to consolidate all 11246 compliance power within the OFCCP itself. The 16 agencies were stripped of enforcement responsibility. The consolidation is now complete, and employment police are being deployed throughout what used to be the Republic.

Don't confuse OFCCP's authority under 11246 with that of the U.S Equal Employment Opportunity Commission (EEOC) under Title VII of the 1964 Civil Rights Act. The agencies are independent of one another and operate under different procedures.

The EEOC neither requires a written Affirmative Action Plan, nor can it debar contractors from government contracts. OFCCP can and does bar from government contracts firms that fail to implement AAP's. The EEOC, on the other hand, "merely" sues employers — not just government contractors — in the federal courts and seeks sanctions against violators. And gets them.

Every government contractor or subcontractor of $50,000 and having 50 employees is required to develop an AAP.

"But," you protest, "why should I be concerned? I'm not a government contractor."

How do you know you're not?

As enforcement revs up, and the happy little bureaucrats sitting in the huge companies nobody really owns, "work" with their opposite numbers—frequently former colleagues—in the government to file the proper AAP's—the OFCCP will be reaching for new worlds to conquer.

It's possible that the reach would even include, for example, a supplier of $50,000 worth of hardware to a group of unrelated government contractors or subcontractors if he has 50 employees.

Manpower Allocations, Wage-Price Guidelines (soon to be Controls, OFCCP and EEOC regulations are the straps of the straitjacket for which the government is measuring you.

WHAT TO DO:

If you employ 50 people and clearly are doing $50,000 a year with the government as a prime or subcontractor, proceed immediately to install your Affirmative Action Plan.

If you don't know how to do it, unless your business can justify an $18,000 a year administrative employee whose job is mainly to achieve compliance with all government regulations, get outside help. It's available from the larger accounting, consulting and law firms. Be sure that whoever you hire is personally working in this field, if not full time, at least consistently enough to be abreast of rapidly changing regulations and enforcement policies.

Even an in-house compliance officer's work should be checked by an outside specialist. Expensive, but a normal direct cost of doing business with the government.

If you have 50 employees and it's conceivable that an aggressive federal employment cop could construe that you are indirectly selling $50,000 of merchandise to the government, consider doing the same as above but on a less urgent basis. You might, for example have your consultant set up the outline of an AAP. Then, should you become more heavily involved in government work—and in the coming war economy, most manufacturing and service businesses will have to be—to remain alive—you can accelerate implementation.

If you clearly have no exposure whatever to 11246, then you're faced with compliance with EEOC. Again, the same outside people can assist you. If you have fewer than 100 employees, the likelihood of being attacked is not great at present. More than 100 employees, you are wide open. Worth the money to build defenses.

Don't get angry. It is cost and a part of doing business. Your competitors have to do the same thing. Read a good paperback called *The Relaxation Response,* by Herbert Benson, M.D.

Finally, every wretched bureaucracy-spawning law originates as an Act of Congress or of your state legislature. The people who vote these laws were elected by the freest of free-enterprisors: Freelance politicians. What did you do last time around to find and work for candidates who would represent your interests, if you know what they are? What are you going to do next time?

# CHAPTER NINE

# How Does It Feel to be Perfect?

"High turnover and absenteeism, low productivity, and a new work ethic characterize today's people management problems. At a special one-day workshop your front line supervisors will learn how they influence these problems . . . how to give proper instructions, effectively communicate feedback, and how to deal with stress and conflict with their employees . . . how to create and maintain a positive work climate."

That is an ad for a seminar that came to the office.

Chances are the fellow selling this seminar sincerely believes he can do all these things in a day—which indicates that he's never owned and run a business. Most of us wrestle with such problems for a lifetime, without trying to figure out what "a new work ethic" means or intruding on that branch of medicine which diagnoses sources of stress and conflict.

This point of view is based upon the unstated, inane assumption that there is such a thing as pure management, or, even pure supervision which can be accomplished by an individual who doesn't know anything about the work or business involved.

According to this notion, it's only necessary to have as much knowledge of human nature as can be learned in a day for any glib nincompoop with the currently fashionable haircut to manage a restaurant, farm, or machine shop without command of the complicated information and skills required.

Today there are more seminars being promoted than at any time in history by desperate characters too lazy to take a job and too unimaginative to go into legitimate business. There's an old saying on college campuses that those who can, do, while those who can't, teach. This idea has now slopped over into the business world.

If seminar performers have no record of making money, why assume they can teach anything to Businessowners? And if, as usual, the promotional literature does not detail what the orators have done to make money for themselves, it's safe to assume they haven't done it.

If they are hired hands in the big corporations that nobody really owns, what can they teach a man who has his own money on the line and who, in effect, bets his roll every morning when he arrives at the vinegar works?

This nonsense originated during a period of rapidly receding history called World War II. Prior to that time, it was understood that you didn't put a man in charge of a pancake house or a plating shop until he had demonstrated thorough knowledge of the work. Supervisory techniques as such did not exist in a vacuum. The boss showed a hand what to do, explained as best he could, then checked the work. The foreman was expected to be forthright in dealing with his crew, not to make promises he couldn't keep, and to fire anybody who did not do the job.

World War II made it necessary to staff factories with thousands of inexperienced hands. Accordingly, a numbing variety of makeshift devices were created, such as isometric in place of mechanical drawings. The so-called art of supervision was invented to replace knowing the job, buttressed by layers of inspectors to throw back bad work. Incidentally, these factories became the womb in which the genetic monster called "Training Director" was gestated.

There's a common misconception that this system worked. It did — if you don't count the cost. The scrap and spoilage in war production achieved such a degree of enormity that IBM has not yet built a computer big enough to calculate it. This was ignored because there was no competition, and besides cost accounting has no role in war. Apart, that is, from filling out forms for the bureaucracies that existed to keep people who were unfit to serve either in the forces or the factories busy in the Office of Price Administration.

It was from this economically barren soil that the weed called pure management sprouted. Cost plus was invented, so the more money that was wasted, the more was charged for the effort of wasting it.

WHAT TO DO:

Now that we're moving into seriously competitive times, forget about new or old work ethics, stress and conflict within employees' hearts, and maintenance of a positive work climate. Just be damn sure that your supervisory employees understand precisely what is to be done and how to do it.

Continuing outside education for supervisory employees is sometimes a justifiable expenditure if it concerns improved work methods that yield measurable improvement in output and/or material and inventory controls. Leave the psychologizing to the shrinks, professors, sociologists, creative writers, and other components of the national overhead.

This notion of continuing education slumbered peacefully among the tax deductible expenses of doctors, lawyers, and teachers since the income tax was invented in 1913. The number of that year makes me superstitious, because that's also when we shifted to the popular election of senators. Downhill ever since.

Will Rogers, incidentally, predicted at the time that the income tax would turn all Americans into crooks. But I digress. As usual.

At any rate, the principle of continuing education was based on the premise that since you had to be graduated from a professional school to practice these old line professions, it made sense to go back for a refresher now and then. New information was constantly coming on stream.

Then, gradually, several things happened, all related to the matter of deductible expenses. First, paid lecturers on business, economics, and trade matters began to appear at conventions. This lent a certain air of credibility to the fun, and gave participants an opportunity to doze in a sitting position between drinking bouts. According to the liquor people, these intermissions resulted in greater overall consumption.

To add legitimacy, politicians — both the elected and appointed kinds — began to soak up — and jack up — the juicier speaking fees. Senators always get the most. Nobody ever pays much attention to their slurred and bumbling ramblings, but the tax laws have not been amended to modify the deductibility of their honoraria, as they like to call their bribes, and from that of other convention expenses.

The next development was the trend toward "professionalizing" service business and the consequent requirement that their members either take courses or attend seminars for which they receive "continuing education units." Accounting and pharmacy, both clearly professional fields came along early, but now we have certified travel agents, certified association executives, and many more.

The third step was a classical example of the "find a need and fill it" theory. This took shape in the explosive growth of the seminar industry. Not many years ago the American Management Association had the field to itself as far as seminars in all respects of administrative management, supervision, and financial analysis seminars were concerned. And that was the ball game.

Now about half the junk mail you throw out every morning is on seminars about anything from advertising to zymurgy for the housewife, with principal emphasis on self-improvement. Most of this foolishness is based on the assumption that if you "improve" yourself per the manner of Dr. X (you are rarely informed what he is a "doctor" of or where he bought the degree), you will grow charm that will sufficiently anesthetize others that they won't notice when you pick their pockets.

I've done seminars myself — although I'm no kind of doctor — and believe me, it beats working.

Undoubtedly you have sent employees to such sessions, as a reward, or additional vacation, the costs of which are deductible to you and not taxable to him. Interesting to note the skill with which conventions, short courses, and seminars are scheduled for hotels designed for the purpose with plenty of recreational facilities, and time between sessions to make adequate use thereof.

Since you own the business, however, you already know all about everything thereto appertaining, and don't need to attend lectures. Still, you hit the annual convention to find out what your competitors are down to, and an occasional round of golf.

In spite of your omniscience, however, modesty requires that you too try to "keep up with developments." Since you realize that most seminars are for jobholders rather than owners, keeping up translates into reading up.

Your unstated assumption in this regard is that journalists and magazine writers and professors have information you need.

The undrained swamp in which you are sinking is not the absurd pile of largely unreadable printed matter on your desk. It's the unwarranted concern, if not downright feeling of guilt, over the fact that you will never read it.

That reaction distracts you from your only legitimate, capitalistic purpose of making money.

The reason there is so much reading matter can be largely attributed to the advertising industry's success in selling wares through newspapers and magazines.

With space sold, it's up to the editorial staff to separate the ads with articles. Considerable skill goes into arranging pages to pull your eye from inside information on pork bellies to ads for underwear and market letters that will make you rich without working.

What information are you looking for? Could this feeling that you ought to read it be a carryover from schoolmarms who prated that whatever you read would be of benefit and that accordingly you should read everything placed in front of you by the mailman? (Like telling your kid to clean his plate?) Or, are you still mentally one of those unusual types who worried if he had not done all his homework?

Do you know what you really want to find out? Can you answer the question, "Why am I reading this?" When you do so honestly, the pile of print dwindles quickly.

The principal use of economic data is to help determine how much to buy and at what price. It is the only decision the owner has to make. Employees can carry out details. The kind of information you need concerns markets, suppliers — including unions and banks — and competitors. As we've talked about in preceeding chapters.

Independent Businessowners every day face a virtual smorgasbord of economic, financial and business data. Much is mental junk food and some merely appeals to the appetite for gossip. Accordingly, at any given time there is much less information than meets the eye, and very little you can use at any particular juncture to help make a buy-sell decision.

Practically all Businessowners proudly announce that they read the *Wall Street Journal* thoroughly every day, when they should merely skim it for anything pertinent to their business. But even on those rare instances when you do find something about your business, it's probably old stuff to you.

The statistics in the *WSJ* — particularly bond, foreign exchange, and commodity quotations — are more important than most of the words.

If you find the articles to be interesting diversions, OK. But don't read them under the delusion you are acquiring anything profitable. The editorials, consisting mainly of unrequested free advice to the government, are not likely to help you make a sound business decision.

Most trade journals are more blatantly contrived to sell advertising than are newspapers. Seldom are they written by a person who had made any money himself in the field. Free lance writers eke out a wretched living rehashing articles for any and all such publications.

When is the last time you can recall actually making a decision, or taking any action as the result of something you read?

The business page of your local paper, which probably carries much of the same statistical data found in the *WSJ*, is likely to be of greater value to you. There you might learn something about local suppliers and markets, especially labor and the interest local banks are getting.

What to do? Recognize newspapers and magazines as businesses like your own. Nothing sacred about the printed page.

Throw out all unread periodicals at the end of the week. Not only will your desk be more manageable but you won't have the overhanging guilt feeling that for some reason you have to get around to all that stuff.

In spite of the widely publicized deficiencies of our postal system, rest assured that the mailman will bring you more tomorrow!

More specifically:

1.   Before reading anything, ask yourself why you are reading it. As I have already suggested, since you won't be able to answer every time, that will reduce your reading load.

2.   *Forbes* is investment oriented. If such financial information will help your business make money, subscribe. Nobody needs both *Business Week* and *U.S. News*. Select the one you prefer. *Nation's Business* serves primarily to reinforce your political views. Unless they are shaky, leave it on the table in your reception office.

3.   Leaf through the *WSJ* for anything that bears on your business, including articles on larger events in the economic ocean, and read only that. It shouldn't take more than five minutes to skim any paper or magazine to ascertain what is important to you

In addition to periodicals, we are all also subject to a smothering cascade of books filled with the unworkable ideas of school teachers, professional writers, and part-time consultants whose only income has been from selling time, regarding every artificial subdivision of business that they have construed by secretly reading what their colleagues published in previous years.

The reason for this desecration of forests is that you and I represent a juicy market for the merchandise. Mostly we buy by mail. It's so easy to fill out a coupon and write a credit card number. I hope that's how you bought a dozen copies of this book for your family and friends.

Publishers know that Businessowners are casting about wildly for answers, or at least for a few ideas that might lead to same.

So we buy. Then what? We start to read. After a chapter or an hour we realize we've been had, dolefully stick the dust cover flap or a scrap of paper into the face where we gave up, and squeeze the volume into the shelf. *When Your Name Is on the Door* is different. You'll read it twice and refer to it many times. Because I earned the right to write it.

Woman Businessowners, being more practical than men—as women are in most other matters—not only don't read those schoolbooks, they also don't read the flood of special books on how women can get ahead in business. Written by journalists, self-promoted activists, and again, by school teachers.

If you must read books—other than for amusement—try Euclid, Plato, and any good text on logic. The amount of money you make is related less to your supply of information than it is to the clarity of your thinking.

There are other exceptions. Take financial data. A client once said, "It's terrible to admit, but I can no longer understand my own financial statement. Maybe I never could but now it's impossible. I hate to appear like a fool in front of my own accountant and our CPA. I tried to read a book on the subject but I'm too old to concentrate on this sort of thing. And please don't tell me to take a night school course."

A night course would, of course have put him—or you—to sleep. And books about financial reporting vary only in degrees of obscurity. If this is your situation, no reason to be embarrassed because you are smart enough to hire men who can do the things you can't do. Since your name is on the door, you obviously know many things incomprehensible to both your accountant and CPA. Engage the latter as a tutor. He knows the information you need and will not consider you foolish. On the contrary, he will say you are very intelligent because you recognize his genius. One of his problems is that not enough clients ask these questions.

Start at the top of the balance sheet, income statement, and statement of changes. Go down each one line by line. Remember, you don't need to learn how to do your CPA's job, but only understand what he has put down.

Also true of the footnotes. Insist that he identify the gobble-dy-gook he put in for his own protection against possible lawsuits.

Do this on a regular basis because rules governing accounting are increasing in number and complexity. You will become one of the few Independent Businessowners who fully understands his reports.

In case your CPA gets carried away with his own professional role, bear in mind that many owners spend their time studying ridiculous expense accounts that they can't do anything about — expense accounts in the operating statement sense as well as in the salesmen sense — instead of paying attention to the great inventory costs, waste and stupidity which really determine their gross losses. Ignore all usually fixed items you can't do much about, concentrate on increasing gross profit, and work at reducing truly variable expenses.

This is one place where corporation officers are ahead of us. Most large companies provide their staffs considerable education in interpreting financial statements. That's because every Division has to find ways to cook its own books to make it appear that they are making their pre-assigned contribution to what the accounting department calls corporate profit.

When you get down to it, Businessowners get continuing education from their own costly errors. Not enough of you study what happens when you do something right — something that works.

Remember the druggist I told you about who discovered a renewed interest in candles and bought up all he could find before his competitors knew what was happening? He made money and discovered a pattern. Now he regularly checks warehouses and wholesalers to find out what old merchandise is still around. He has since done well in bicycle accessories and pine cones. At the time he found these job lots, nobody else wanted them. He saw markets coming up. Pine cones? For decorator purposes. Especially at Christmas.

A manufacturer found a problem during one of his regular field trips. On the plane home, he personally developed solutions. Now he hires more employees to handle the administrative work he was carrying and does more quick analysis of design problems in the field. He knows enough not to spend his time on design details, but feeds ideas into his so-called engineering department, which is really a bunch of glorified draftsmen.

This fellow started as a quick and dirty engineer, got fired a couple of times because he wasn't much good on detail. Because he couldn't hold a job has since built and is continuing to build a business based upon his skill at finding out what he does that works well, and repeating the process.

Again, analyze your own experience. See what you did right in order that you can do more of it. Stop the oft-reiterated nonsense about analyzing your mistakes. All that does is make you repeat them over and over. Negative conditioning.

If you haven't analyzed your own experience, you're no better off than the general's mule. The general said his mule had been through thirty campaigns, but he didn't know any more about military strategy now than at the beginning. Or the bookkeeper who claimed to have had thirty years of experience, but who in reality had had one year's experience thirty times.

I said earlier the most important thing a businessowner or anyone else can do is think straight, or learn to think straighter. This is hard work, which is the reason very few people do it.

The first question to ask yourself — easier to ask than answer — is what is it you want to do, when, and for what purpose. This gets into that tiresome expression about "arranging your priorities" that is so dear to the heart of lecturers on how to do everything in the world, but who, themselves, can't do anything but talk about it.

So stop thinking about time and start thinking about what should be done first, what should be done second, the purpose for which these things are to be done, and the results you fully intend to attain thereby.

After you do everything necessary to accomplish your objectives, then you either set out some new ones or go out and get drunk.

All of these lectures, books, articles, seminars, etc. about time are full of gimmicks and unstated assumptions. One of the most insulting is that the same methods and series of tricks are equally useful to all people. Another is that businessowners can be treated as if they were production workers — on something of an industrial engineering basis.

If you've read me this far, you know that a businessowner's effectiveness — "use of time" — cannot be measured by counting or weighing the work he has done. He hasn't drilled so many holes or stacked up crates of apricots. The only measure of the owner's efforts are to be found in the much touted, little understood bottom line. The one after which you don't subtract anything else.

One of the most egregious recommendations is that everyone should always have something to read in his pocket, or in the glove compartment of his car. The theory seems to be that such disjointed reading would be beneficial to everybody.

A few years ago there was a fad encouraging people to perform isometric exercises during idle moments. The assumption here was that everyone would be benefitted by performing these contortions, and there was no danger of being arrested for making faces in a hotel lobby while waiting for your wife to come out of the ladies' room.

Another popular recommendation is to "save time" by dictating while driving your car. I knew a fellow once who did that in Los Angeles. He hit the back of a cement truck, the driver of which didn't know it until a traffic cop advised him. Just kept going. He had a lot of time thereafter in the hospital to think things over. My friend couldn't dictate, however, because his face was smashed in.

Then there is the favorite of many consultants, which is to zero in on organizing paper work. They seem to feel that if you follow their system of doing so, that that in itself will "save time" or make you more efficient.

Again, the unstated assumption there is that reshuffling papers is profitable. No evidence exists that any of these assumptions are valid.

Your purpose is not to organize time or even to organize work, unless you are a production worker for a manufacturing enterprise. The real objective is to organize yourself to work on your own initiative rather than by reacting to the most recent crisis with the objective of making a targeted amount of money. You're not paid for filling out forms.

Another redundantly marketed approach to getting things done is through a peculiar sort of mysticism of the type written about by Norman Vincent Peale, Napoleon Hill, and other great creative writers. There's a constant stream of promotional material for rehashes of this sort of thing.

Oddly enough, they are right in one respect but not necessarily for the reason they give. These inspirational writers say something to the effect that "you can do, be, or get anything you want." They usually define the process, however, as wishing for it, mystically, and forming mental pictures while sitting on your rump, rather than working at white heat.

That leads to the basic complaint of practically all businessowners, which is as if they are the only ones in the outfit with a sense of urgency. Usually true, and a good thing too. Most businesses still small enough to be owned and run by one person, or possibly a partnership or family, simply do not have room for more than one individual with a sense of urgency.

Possibly a few supervisory employees should have half a sense of urgency. Otherwise everyone would get in each other's way. There would be collisions.

We started this chapter asking how it feels to be perfect. If you weren't, you wouldn't own the business. If you have doubts now and then, all you need to do is think.

# CHAPTER TEN

# Truman's Half Truth

A million years ago when I was an urchin in the public schools of Oakland and Berkeley — they're in California — the silly, tenured crones called teachers repeated ad nauseam that any boy could grow up to become President. That Coolidge and Hoover were in office did not deter them.

Then a series of tenth raters came along and proved the old biddies were right. Except for Eisenhower, we haven't had a President since 1932 who put the U.S. system above that of the USSR.

One of them was the ignorant errand boy of the country's most corrupt political machine — the Pendergast outfit down in Kansas City. This little scamp couldn't even keep his name on the door of a haberdashery. The word is out of date. Means they stock men's clothing — stock it — don't know how to sell it, as this pint-sized squirt with a brain to match demonstrated.

Bartlett to the contrary notwithstanding, you never knew for sure who said what. But Roosevelt's final joke on the American people gets credit for the wise sounding comment, "The buck stops here." Whether he or his secretary really said it is immaterial.

Now, for reasons known only to them, the mysterious employers of such molders of public opinion as TV anchor men and syndicated columnists have awarded Harry Truman a posthumous promotion to the level of George Washington. Accordingly, it's going to be hard for those of you too young to have heard his incoherent ramblings in person to accept the fact that not only was Truman a twerp generally — which we haven't time to go into here — but he was merely half right in the only putative quotation for which he is remembered.

Sure, the buck stops at your desk. You've always known that.

The point that frequently eludes the Businessowner is that the buck starts there.

You create everything, specifically including all your messes. The business is your creation. Almost a begotten child. You've determined both its heredity and environment. So when hens return to roost, don't treat them as foundlings you're stuck with. You sent them out in the first place.

Which means — taking a thread I dropped somewhere along the line — the probability of your keeping your name on the door varies directly with your ability to recognize that your employees are that and nothing more. They are the help. The hired hands, with a head thrown in now and then. And your employees are not basically different from other jobholders — regardless of the rank you bestow on them or of how many other employees they supposedly supervise.

Colloquial wisdom has it for example, that large corporations are rife with company politics, but that independently owned businesses are not so afflicted.

Rubbish. Whenever more than two people are in one outfit, probably starting at age two, they form warring groups. If three kids play together, two sooner or later will gang up against the third, and after a while, they'll shift and a different one will be odd moppet out.

The notion that the employees of independently owned businesses are not playing politics among themselves and against the boss possibly derives from the fact that the owner himself does not have to waste energy in such games.

You have the privilege—sometimes lost by stumbling over your own feelings, prejudices, and unstated assumptions—of making all business decisions for business reasons. You don't have to worry how others may react. Of course, you may do so anyway, which is your loss.

Most of you became owners at a comparatively early age, and to a large degree have forgotten or never knew what it's like to be an employee. A surprising number of owners go into business directly from the ranks, so to speak.

They were mechanics of one type or another, lawyers, cooks, pharmacists, truck drivers, dentists, janitors, physicians, policemen, or accountants before scrounging up a few dollars and taking the plunge. Skipped the intermediate step of being a so-called management employee, and therefore never were directly involved in company politics.

So owners don't always realize that their pet supervisory employees are members of informal guerilla gangs that attempt to get higher positions, easier working conditions, and more money from you by complicated and not-so-complicated schemes unrelated to doing a good job of work.

EXAMPLES:

A gear manufacturer with half-a-dozen offices around the country felt his intelligence was insulted when he received phone calls or memos from all six District Managers within a two-week period recommending similar changes in credit policy. Easier terms, of course.

He hopes that in time his men will develop a little more sophistication.

Then we have individuals who try to curry favor by inviting your attention to the other fellow's weaknesses. "Damning by faint praise."

Like the Chief Engineer (fancy word for overpaid draftsman, who through obscure mental processes creates a parts

numbering system that only he can pretend to understand),
who says of the Manufacturing Manager: "Jack really gets the
work out. He's on the job long after everyone else from the day
shift has left. Sometimes I kind of wonder whether all that
push takes enough account of quality . . . "

Or, the Sales Manager who advises you after this same Chief
Engineer has returned from accompanying the Boston man on
an important call: "Walter was very helpful in handling some
of the technical questions the Zilch Company had. Trouble is,
he seems to have committed us to several changes on Model
Z-14-B. I sure hope they won't be too costly . . . "

Nor should we ignore the Purchasing Agent or Quality Control Manager who stumbles across an article written by a college professor whose experience has been limited to summertime consulting on "organizational development" in companies that nobody really owns, and where everybody is an
employee, on the beauties of the "Works Manager" concept.
The obvious implication being that the fellow who handed the
article to the boss should be Works Manager.

WHAT TO DO:

1. Recognize that a good clique-builder has talent to influence men. May not be exactly leadership, but gets results.
Particularly useful in developing a national sales force that has
to hit various offices of the same customer outfits around the
country.

2. Be alert to any comment by an employee regarding the
work of any other employee, good or bad. Or personal gossip.
Ninety-nine times out of a hundred, no matter how cleverly
expressed, it's designed to make the tale-bearer look better in
your eyes at the expense of the other fellow.

3. Waste no ergs attempting to stop this sort of thing. Can't
be done.

4. Be sure you have told all employees what is expected of
them, how you judge them, and that they understand what
you have told them. Then follow through. Develop objective,
measureable standards of performance. The more clearly

supervisory employees know what is required of them, and how they are judged, the less time they will squander on amateur Machiavellian maneuverings. More on this in Chapters XI and XII.

Independent Businessowners make money when they build an organization on purpose, and lose money when they build one by accident, let it grow like Topsy, and refuse to dismantle it.

The building process begins — either deliberately or unintentionally — when you give an employee authority to spend your money, and/or when you hire one to do non-productive work.

Usually the first step is to make a productive employee non-productive by appointing him a supervisor, and assume he knows what to do and how to do it. Since your biggest expenditures are for employees — wages plus other compensation — the minute you appoint a supervisor, you in effect give him authority to write checks for amounts that you cannot control. Sure, you established the rates, but he governs how much you get in return. True in any business.

Manufacturing, of course, has special non-productive employment costs in what are euphemistically called engineering departments. People paid to draw things that practical mechanics have trouble making, and when they do, don't work.

Conspicuous in every enterprise from mining to merchandising is the unstated assumption that supervisory employees are exercising their responsibilities when they are merely wandering around the shop.

In the huge, public companies that nobody really owns and frequently nobody really runs, you sometimes find so-called internal consultants whose function is to teach their jobs to straw bosses whose superiors haven't done so because they are too busy guarding their political flanks.

You can spare yourself that expense.

Normal overhead is mainly hiring people to keep track of what you've done and to fill out government forms. Bookkeepers or accountants, depending on how much you pay them. The problem with these types is that they are more interested in pretending to comply with accounting rules they only dimly apprehend than in providing you with information useful in making buy and sell decisions.

Employees hired to assure your compliance with employment, environmental, and safety regulations constitute direct, inescapable costs that must be built into your prices. Your competitors are in the same boat.

The weakness throughout overhead structures is that people either don't know what to do, don't know how to do it, or don't have enough to do and so spend their time politicking.

WHAT TO DO:

Before appointing a supervisor, ask yourself whether you can direct more workers yourself. And before authorizing employees to spend your money, consider whether it would be more profitable to handle that chore personally and drop some other diversions.

Remember, if you manage all — or even half — of a production or operating force, you eliminate the expense of a supervisor's compensation and the consequences of his incompetence.

If your outfit has grown to a size legitimately requiring supervisory employees, the trap to avoid is that of assuming that they know what to do all day.

They should:
1. Assign work.
2. Instruct people how to do it.
3. Check the work.
4. Make corrections.

The fact that a man may have been the best welder, clerk or clockmaker does not mean he can perform those four key tasks. Teach him. We'll be coming back to these ideas for the rest of this compendium.

When you recognize that you've made an error in selecting a supervisory employee, the trap to avoid is that of hiring a replacement for him, then giving the new boy less work and more money.

For example, Oscar the factory owner decided that Ajax, his Chief Inspector should do more work. Note, I did not say add on more responsibility.

The Chief Inspector's job was primarily within the factory. His department was well organized. Quality control in the plant was excellent.

The problem was with buy-outs. The number of feeder shops was increasing, but the quality of their production was uneven. Usually it was necessary for Ajax to wait for hurried shipments of parts or subassemblies before checking them and finding problems.

So, observing the good job Ajax had done in organizing his department, Oscar called him in and filled him with the trade's version of compliments, kisses, and gin. Gave him a company car and a list of suppliers. Ajax was not only to check their work but show them how to control quality.

The Inspector started the added duties with a bang, but after a year, it became clear that he simply was not doing the outside job, and in-plant quality was also slipping.

Oscar expostulated, cajoled, tried to help, threatened, jumped up and down and flapped his wings, but still Ajax did not rise to the occasion.

Oscar phoned me to find out whether men might be available. Since Ajax had failed on the outside job, he was going to fire him, hire a new internal Chief Inspector and also another fellow to handle supplier quality control and in addition take on some purchasing negotiations with the feeder shops. This man would command a higher salary then Ajax.

When I suggested he use Ajax for one of the two jobs, Oscar replied, "Why, when he has already failed on the outside?"

Oscar was ignoring the fact that Ajax failed on the outside while also doing the in-house quality control work.

So you can see the trap — the classical error — of offering an easier job to a new employee and destroying any possible basis for comparing performance. Oranges and apples.

In this connection, bear in mind that the outsider always looks better than the man whose shortcomings you know. A stranger comes in wearing his best suit, acting the suave and knowledgeable part. You are ignorant of his weaknesses, but the impression he makes is one of freshness and competence.

Imagine how your own Ajax would look applying for a job. Instead of the inadequate individual who irks you, he would change to a properly dressed gentleman meeting a businessman of only slightly more exalted rank.

WHAT TO DO:

Define jobs realistically. Don't throw out the baby with the bathwater.

Going a little further into the task of replacing a supervisor, of all the mud holes in the path of the Independent Businessowner, the Received Wisdom that owners must promote from within is the gooey-est.

Probably because it's the path of least resistance. Then you rationalize, telling yourself it's better to promote somebody whose weaknesses you know than to gamble on an unknown qualtity. Also, there is the old bugaboo of employee morale.

There seems to be an unstated assumption throughout the land that if you bring in an outsider when a good job opens up, the production or clerical workers will get discouraged and do even less than they are doing now — if that's possible.

This may be true of one or two people who could conceivably have expected to get the break. Since you know who they are, tell them why they were not advanced, and what they have to do to qualify for the next opening. Should they quit, or sulk to force you to fire them, good riddance.

If you have a top hand to bring in from the outside, obviously you're not going to sacrifice the money he can make for you just to keep a man who is unhappy where he is, and is at the same time unwilling or unable to prepare for more responsibility.

As far as the majority of employees under the new supervisor are concerned, it's his job to handle them and if he is as good as you think he is — that's why you hired him — he'll probably get more work out of them than his predecesor.

Aside from the questionable philosophy of promoting from

within because it's the easiest thing to do, there are two other reasons Businessowners all over the country give with tiresome monotony for following this practice.

Seniority, oddly enough was not originally a union demand. Too many owners suffer from vague feelings that they ought to recognize a long-time employee. If this is your state of mind, and you're not convinced that the old-timer is really the best person for the heavier job, give him a raise or a bonus. Chances are he knows perfectly well he should stay at his present level, will appreciate your gesture somewhat, and the cash a great deal more.

Maybe this is a good time to remind you that in spite of the learned tomes perennially published by professors that list all the motivations for working other than for the money, we have yet to find a business capable of keeping employees without paying them.

Again, your attitude governs employee behaviour. If you are practical — not dreamy-eyed — they'll work a day for a day's wages.

The other standard reason for elevating an employee to supervisory status is that he's the best accountant, machinist, welder, salad chef, or meatcutter in the shop. This has nothing to do with supervisory ability. Does not mean he's interested in teaching, organizing, and follow-up. Nor signify that he wants to — or can — deal directly with you, or if your business is large enough, with a boss who reports directly to a general manager or to you.

How to decide whether an employee should be promoted: Be skeptical of the man who asks what he must do to advance. Favor the fellow who takes on responsibility without being asked to do so. The one who just naturally helps the person at the next desk or machine. The unofficial leader.

If you're unionized, open-mindedly evaluate shop stewards. Since they've been elected, they must have some leadership ability. Be warned, however, that stewards who make foreman often turn out supertough on the men, and continually challenge the union. One extreme to the other.

WHAT TO DO:

When you need to appoint a new foreman, office manager, branch manager, purchasing agent, etc.:

1.　Redefine the job. Don't assume it will or should be the same as the previous or a parallel job-holder. List all the things he'll have to do all day.

2.　Determine the skills or knowledge necessary to do these things.

3.　Write out the questions you will ask applicants to ascertain whether they have the skill and knowledge. If you don't interview from a check list, you'll forget to ask an important question.

4.　Interview as many applicants as possible from employment agencies and newspaper ads. Don't be afraid to recruit from suppliers, customers and competitors.

5.　Check with previous employers — owners if possible — personally. People are so gun-shy on this lately that you may have to do so face to face. Worth the time. The higher the job, the more you stand to make if your judgment is right, and the more to lose if you're wrong.

6.　Before offering the job, be sure the applicant you select knows in detail what he will have to do all day if he gets the job.

You'll notice that everything I've been saying regarding the way in which you see your employees to determine whether you are making a profit on what they cost you has ignored psychology, astrology, palmistry, and human relations. We'll get into these and other techniques of hiring, handling, and firing the help in later chapters in greater detail.

Suffice it to say for the moment that companies that are people oriented are in the same situation as naval officers whose cadets are being taught seamanship on the basis of their relationship with the crew, while paying no attention to the condition of the ocean, the ship, the weather, and how to operate the ship.

People problems are created by mush-headed management much in the same way as people who might rub a very slight rash and work it up into a major infection.

The whole people orientation idea in business seems to be the result of what looks like a conspiracy among psychologists, educators, educationists, and various government functionaries who couldn't think of much else to do. Obviously the deliberate conspiracy theory is nonsense, but the way the thing took hold in business for a number of years lends it some credibility.

Let's come at this another way, to help you see it rightly. As I've already reminded you, chances are that you jumped from clerk or mechanic to small business owner. You arranged financing, got legal and accounting advice, put aside enough money to live for a year while your business developed, and worked with thorough dedication. Success. But suddenly you found yourself with an organization.

You probably never worked in an organization in the sense of being a boss and having a boss simultaneously.

Now you find that you have organizational or what some people term people problems. And that is a way to avoid facing facts. If your employees are not doing things the way you want them to, it's because you have not instructed them properly. You don't have people problems. You have problems in your own mind deciding what to do and how to do it.

And why do I hammer at the word "employee," and fight off the word "people?" Because the latter, especially expressed in "my people," or "my guys," implies slaveholding at worst and benevolent royalty or dictatorship at best.

Your employees are that only, and only after they've punched in and before they've punched out. Cleanse your mind of any other notion. Then you won't be confused at their reactions.

When relationships among employees — up, down and sidewise — are smooth and a state of equilibrium appears to have been reached, that's bad.

The reason it is bad is that it means either that nobody is being sufficiently aggressive and thereby running into other people, or that employees are pussyfooting around one another to avoid conflict.

Business can be sacrificed on the altar of harmony as well as on the altar of principle. Harmony per se is not a good thing. Employees as well as owners increase their strengths in conflict and competition.

The stuffiest Businessowner is the individual who says the only real pleasure left in business is building men. I've not yet heard anyone speak of building women, but there are always new things to look forward to.

It is true that helping employees to improve their skills — not themselves! — is a source of satisfaction, but don't try to play God. You have a less demanding job. It is simply to earn a suitable return on your investment.

Speaking of supervisory employees, in an organization very few people will give the same kind of information to their subordinates that they wish to receive from their superiors. The Golden Rule is not practiced any more in business than in other aspects of life. Employees at all levels refuse to treat their subordinates the way they want their superiors to treat them.

This matter will receive more emphasis in the chapters to come, but as you now realize, it's impractical to analyze one phase of the owner's job — in this case, the fact that the buck starts as well as ends with you — without pointing out its infringement on others.

For example, a client who manufactures hydraulic pumps complained that although his suppliers were slow, when he got on the phone or plane himself he got results. Wanted to know what kind of expeditor to hire — what qualifications such a man should have.

The answer was any man with basic experience in the industrial field to whom he, the owner, would relinquish authority to make whatever commitments were necessary to get action from suppliers.

This owner, like many of you, had by his actions over the years, convinced his suppliers — and probably his customers too, that he was the only one in the outfit to be taken seriously.

As you've learned by this time, two of the most significant components of your attitude toward the source of your heaviest expenses — employees — is that number one, you are not in the people business, and number two, you have no investment in your employees. Thanks to Abraham Lincoln, you can't sell them. And thanks to the IRS, you can't depreciate them either.

All you can do is spend more money on them. This logically leads to your questioning attitude toward the funny person who asks for more responsibility.

Responsibility cannot be given. It can only be assumed. An employee who asks for responsibility indicates his inability to handle it.

It means reacting to everything that goes wrong as if it were his fault. Means he must stick his neck out. Responsibility is a state of mind. Example: If a flower pot falls on your head as you walk down the street, you think, "I shouldn't have been there." The responsible individual never blames anyone else or the world for what happens to him.

So the question here is why don't more employees assume responsibility? The answer is that while 95 percent don't want to, you've discouraged the few who do by jumping on them on the rare occasions they tried sticking their neck out. An instinctive reaction on your part. But the buck, nevertheless, started with you.

If you have noticed that some of your salaried people waste a good deal of time trying to find out what others are doing, what you're planning to do next, etc., and have attributed this political activity to increase in your staff, you're off base. You've always had company politics but weren't aware of it.

While you can't stop employees from yapping, you can reduce the need for this amateur sleuthing by explaining your plans and policies—assuming you know what they are. You might also tell all employees exactly what their duties are, how they are judged, and what they have to do in order to get a raise.

Again, you started the ball game by not explaining in advance.

Admittedly, this matter of being the author of your own problems probably as a result of your basic temperament is hard to grasp. Down in San Diego a gentleman by the name of Richard Russell publishes a newsletter called the *Dow Theory Letter*. In my judgement it's the best technical letter on the securities market in the country, and it's written in plain English. Incidentally, I don't know Mr. Russell, have never met him, and have no business connection with him, but because he does such a good job, I'm glad to hand him this free ad.

In one of his semi-monthly epistles he made the amazing observation—I think with a straight face—that some people are just destined not to make money in the market, because of their Karma. Karma is a mystical idea that I think is based on the theory of reincarnation. You've done something bad in a previous life so you're being punished in this one.

If I read this in any other investment letter, I would have cancelled my subscription immediately on the theory that the writer was nuts. But maybe this Karma thing is not as crazy as it sounds, in spite of the fact that evidence of reincarnation is scanty. A tremendous number of Businessowners seem to have attitudes that could have only come from a previous lifetime. Even some entrepreneurs under 40 don't seem to be aware of the fact that owning a business does not imply ownership of employees. Judging from the fact that they appear to expect supervisors or other so-called middle-management types to work countless hours without pay as some sort of privilege.

They expect these folks to have the same proprietary attitude towards the business the owner has, and seem to be in a complete fuddle when such people prefer to work in their back yard rather than drive down to the vinegar works on weekends. Probably these owners would go completely berserk if they realized how many of "their guys" were working at moonlighting jobs, evenings and weekends.

Observations like this, over a period of years in the consulting business, make me wonder whether Mr. Richard Russell has something. It's hard to find other explanations for ancient attitudes in young Businessowners.

Finally, consulting with dozens of owners, I very often get a response something like this: "Brodie, you seem to make a lot of sense and basically I agree with you. The trouble is I don't seem to be able to run my business in the totally businesslike way you advise. What's wrong?"

The answer is that if you have this problem, your competition is not yet tough enough. When they catch up, you'll catch on.

By using these methods, you will hire the most profitable employees. And if you treat your present gang as I have suggested in this chapter and will lay out in detail in the next, you will have less hiring to do.

But remember — you are hiring help — not building men, or women, or contributing to the betterment of society or giving people an opportunity to express themselves or to actualize themselves, whatever the hell that means.

# CHAPTER ELEVEN

# Hiring the Help

Don't interview another applicant . . . until you've read this.

Independent Businessowners base interviewing procedures on the unstated assumption that they know how to do it. There's no connection between knowing your business, or what has to be done in a given job, and knowing how to interview.

We say this because the stream of complaints from all kinds of businesses about how hard it is to hire help, high turnover, employees quitting after a week, etc., indicates poor hiring practices.

The business reason for interviewing is to select employees to do specific jobs. Non-business, or psychological reasons are to puff yourself up, bully someone, etc.

Businessowners are no different from corporate bureaucrats in using interviews for non-business purposes. Not by deliberate thought-out plan, but just human cussedness.

Two traps await the businessowner who does his own hiring. First is using the interview for personal reasons. Second is trying to hire for something other than the job that is open, based on the myth that when the President of Standard Oil retires, a new office boy is hired. Or that every employee is a management trainee, whatever that means.

It's just as unprofitable to look for future managers when hiring clerks or machine tenders as it is to believe an applicant for a clerical or production job who say he wants a job with an opportunity for advancement.

If he hasn't advanced already, chances are he won't, and is setting himself up for the same short term with you he's had elsewhere. Costs you money and does him no good.

That's because the applicant who has been working at ordinary jobs knows in his heart that's what he is going to continue to do, but feels he ought to tell himself and anyone who will listen that he has ambition. The minute he realizes he has no more chance of handling the harder jobs in your shop than with previous employers, he's lost face to himself, and does not want to lose it in front of you. So he quits.

The only employees to whom you should offer an opportunity of advancement are those who have been working for you long enough for you to know one another.

Tell a prospective employee that the only opening is the job under discussion. If he asks about advancement, say that while it may be theoretically possible, there is little likelihood as far as you can see. You'll take good applicants off the hook, and get some acceptable workers.

Since most hiring is based on an interview, here are four things to do before you meet the applicants:

1.  Redefine the job. Don't assume it will or should be the same as the previous or parallel jobholder. You might even find you don't need to fill it, and thereby save a salary.
2.  Determine the skills or knowledge necessary to do that job.
3.  Write down the questions you have to ask to find out whether the applicant has those skills or knowledge. If you don't, you'll forget something. Anyone running a business or a major department thereof, and who is not a full-time personnel interviewer, cannot expect to remember all the questions.

4.  If questions alone won't do it, establish the practical tests that you will use. Not psychological tests, which I will eviscerate shortly.

Now here are five things to do and keep in mind when you see an applicant:

1.  Before asking any questions, describe the job. Be sure he knows what he will have to do all day and how his work — not he, himself — will be judged. The standards you use. If the work is measurable, explain. If it's strictly your judgment or the judgment of a supervisory employee, make that clear.
2.  Bend over backwards to be honest and truthful in explaining what the job really consists of — all the things he will be expected to do — including sweeping up. Give full details regarding the pay, hours, benefits, etc. Again, speak only in terms of the specific job to be filled. These two steps will eliminate many applicants, so you will not have to bother questioning them.
3.  If the applicant is still interested, ask the questions that you have written down. OK for them to be on a sheet of paper in front of you, or even to place a copy in front of him. Since you're going to ask them, they're not secret.
4.  If the replies lead you to other questions, nothing wrong with that, but return to the script as soon as possible.
5.  Don't confuse an employment interview with a police investigation. You are trying to get information, not trap somebody.

Applicants seldom lie, but often exaggerate or kid themselves. Trust your instincts and hunches. If you get a negative reaction — or suspect you are getting lies, end the session. Remember your business reason for conducting the interview.

And don't be afraid to check references. Be persistent in questioning former employers.

But suppose you "haven't time" to interview. If you believe that re-read Chapters IX and X. If you still delegate hiring to supervisory employees with nice titles, consider that the childlike faith of many corporate executives and some Independent Businessowners in professional interviews is touching indeed.

For example, take the situation where you need a man who will grab the ball and run with it, have nobody in your shop, and don't know anyone on the outside. So you engage an Executive Search firm who proceeds to do what they do best — search.

Eventually, they present two or three possibilities. They've interviewed these birds in depth and have made what investigations they could. Usually the candidates are employed, so it's difficult for the head hunters to check with present employers. Based on their interviews — sometimes by professional interviewers — they say that all their candidates meet your requirements. Pick the fellow who appeals to you.

You hire a man. He demonstrates all the technical ability needed, but in spite of the fact that the write-up would lead to the opposite conclusion, he does not demonstrate the essential initiative — the sense of urgency — you're looking for. You specified a man who can get things done and you've been handed one who will do exactly what he is told to do — and do it well.

Reminds me of the week in which I met separately with heads of three different businesses. Southern California retail chain, Pennsylvania electronic equipment distributor, and multi-plant producer of engineered products for the petroleum industry.

What did they have in common? The need for men who could function on their own initiative. Who are enthusiastic about their work and committed to it.

Two of these clients who had either recruited candidates themselves or hired head hunters to do so, had afterwards engaged psychiatrists or psychologists — professional interviewers — to study them.

No question that some psychotherapists and police detectives can provide fair estimates as to the circumstances under which an individual will work well, and those under which he might blow sky high. Everything about a man except what you really need to know—what he has actually done. All the legitimate professionals in the world are as useful in this respect as your garden variety astrologer.

The findings of the brightest shrink in the world may be useful but are of necessity incomplete. To paraphrase an old saying, "There's such divinity doth hedge psychology." You're interested in a man's performance, not his subconscious or his skill in handling so-called expert interlocutors.

WHAT TO DO? Two things.

First, constantly recruit. Whether you have jobs open or not. Don't wait for someone to quit, get fired, or run over before looking for replacements. Part of your job. Essential to be continually alert to individuals working for competitors, similar companies, suppliers, and customers.

Second, investigate. When you are serious about taking on a man for his qualities from the neck up, investigate yourself or have him checked out by a firm that will go through the tedious business of finding out what he actually did in previous jobs or does in his present firm. It's necessary to inquire not only of his supervisors, but subordinates, suppliers and customers.

This is the kind of dogged effort similar to what the FBI used to do checking prospective government employees. Laborious, time-consuming, and expensive.

But not as expensive as hiring the wrong man.

While we're on this matter of acquiring people with brains, the business of interviewing wives of potential executives and/or trainees is as profound a fallacy as may be observed in the entire galaxy of stupidities comprising the American business practice in general and personnel procedures in particular.

As the late Thomas Wolfe might have said, "Only the dead can do this." No guy living understands women that well. Besides the critters change from time to time. Also, women change husbands.

Psychological tests, sometimes known as psychometric

devices, have a definite place in any well run Personnel Department. That place is in the wastebasket.

There has never been a psychological test of the type designed for hiring employees not based upon a common situation. That situation consists of a table, a chair, pencil and paper. Normally, there is also an untrained person administering the test to an individual who is either jaundiced or terrified.

No evidence has been adduced that these factors have been wiped out through the ingenious mathematical and statistical techniques evolved by the hairbrained, intellectually phthisic types found in the basements of University buildings.

In plain English, the whole damn thing depends upon a person's ability to take a school-type test. They have no practical validity and if they have any statistical reliability or internal consistency, such indices cannot obviously reflect anything other than the individual's ability to take a psychological test.

If the job applicant has had 10 jobs in the last 9 years, he will probably have become proficient in this art. A bright young fellow applying for his first job might well be scared to death and flunk the test.

Any well seasoned job applicant or ex-serviceman knows that these tests depend upon three areas of mental activity: vocabulary, arithmetic, and spatial relationships. I am sure that you have met dozens of blathering, sententious idiots who know most of the words in the English language, have mastered the basics of arithmetic, and who worked in an aircraft assembly plant during one of the wars long enough to read simple shop blueprints and isometric drawings to classify himself as a genius in the aforementioned three areas, but who cannot think his way in from the rain. In wartime, these people usually become Second Lieutenants.

Producing and selling tests is a business, even if done through an allegedly "non-profit" corporation whose supervisory employees draw down compensation well above the minimum wage, with expense accounts and perks to match.

These salesmen are in the same trade as other purveyors of

office supplies who plod through office buildings where they have bribed the security staff, or pile up profitable mileage driving around industrial areas. To hire help based on their tests would be as clever as managing your portfolio on the basis of a correspondence course in investing.

About 20 years ago a man named Caryl Chessman was executed at San Quentin, after spending nearly twelve years on death row. According to the late Carolyn Anspacher, in an article she wrote for the *San Francisco Chronicle*, "Prison officials say that when he first was admitted to San Quentin, Chessman attained a very respectable 123 to 124 on his intelligence tests. Subsequently, they say, he 'manipulated' the examinations until he brought his IQ scores up to the ingenious level of 143."

If you still like tests, bear in mind that today all tests and examinations are opposed by the government as a result of pressure from minorities and volunteer advocates of equal opportunity regulations. For example, the California State Bar examination has been changed to reduce the essay type and increase the number of dart-throwing questions as a result of pressure from minorities. So there will be more "lawyers" for the government to hire.

Although psychological tests as such are dumb, there may be good tests for measuring such specific skills as typing. You get into real trouble, however, with tests designed to measure personal qualities such as personality, leadership, etc.

This business of hiring the help, managing and motivating it has all been elevated to an absurd degree of complexity which has resulted in businessowners and their supervisory employees doing much more personnel work then necessary. It also, of course, leads directly into running the business for the benefit of your employees, rather than for your own benefit.

Talk all you want to and listen to all the lectures you can about recruiting and selecting employees, surround yourself by modern mysticism of academic and popular psychology, it still simply comes down to hiring the help. Just thinking about it in those terms will simplify the matter.

Before you hire anybody you have to have applicants from whom to select. Where do you get them? The best, of course, are those who come around and ask for a job. If people are not knocking at your door, you have to go out and look for them. That's called active recruiting.

Before you spend your money and energy trying to persuade people to apply for work at your place, analyze why it's not already happening. Why aren't people applying?

You might say it's because in your particular line of business, there's already full employment, and the unskilled are sufficiently subsidized by the government that they have no incentive to look for work. These are comfortable assumptions for Businessowners to sit on as sort of a pad under their rump. But as Gershwin said, "It ain't necessarily so."

I don't care whether you're hiring butchers or tool-makers — and I know some embittered manufacturing types will say there is no difference — there's always turnover. Employees quit, get fired, or laid off for any number of reasons which their former employers might consider good and you would find bad. Or vice versa. There's always flux and movement in every line of work.

Also, it may surprise you to know, since you have been off the street for a long time, that there is a street in every occupation, trade, profession or what have you. Regardless what kind of business you are in, people who hold jobs in other shops similar to yours know about you. Talk about you. Jobholders, no less than businessowners, get together and talk shop. But the shop the jobholders talk relates to jobs at different outfits in the field rather than to the business itself.

Such elevated colloquies are carried on, not only in beer joints and union halls, but in homes and over backyard fences. Also husbands, wives and POSSLQ's* constantly keep an eye

---

*POSSLQ: Person of opposite sex sharing living quarters. Credit for authorship of this acronym goes to Louis Rukeyser of Wall Street Week. I think he said he got the idea from the census form.

out for job opportunities in which cell-mates might be interested.

This grapevine is going 24 hours a day in the United States because so many people work swing and graveyard shifts. All the way from baby-sitters to electronic engineers, heart-surgeons, and a few who are cross-licensed in all three rackets.

So if these people are changing jobs, between jobs or thinking about changing jobs, how is it they haven't checked your place out? Probably because it has a lousy reputation as a place to work.

Now you're going to throw up your hands and say that you pay as well or better than others in the business, that your benefits are greater, etc. All probably true. Still, none of these things address the primary reasons people don't like to work for you, probably including quite a few of your own employees who are even now, when they're off sick, out interviewing for other jobs.

Assuming that pay, benefits, and physical working conditions are roughly comparable, people get fed up with a job because they are not clear as to what is required of them, are not sure how their work is being judged, are never recognized for doing a good job, don't receive respect, and they don't know what the hell is going on.

One of the most frequent unstated assumptions of Businessowners and of their supervisory employees is that jobholders know what is wanted of them. Even the most experienced machinist, welder, pharmacist, or check-out clerk doesn't know all the peculiarities that characterize your operation.

Don't know whether you want quality or the appearance of it. Whether you want speed in terms of results and output or the conspicuous expenditure of energy and motion. Inadequate effort is made to explain and re-explain these matters at regular intervals.

Not only is it to your financial advantage to take infinite pains to review all of these things—and nobody will be insulted by your being too elementary—but also to tell employees, not only when they are hired, but from time to time during the course of their employment what kind of work and how much of it is expected within what period of time and how you will judge the results. And try, try hard to judge the work, not the worker.

The reason for this is the phenomenon that might be labeled mental drift on the part of owners. You have a way of changing objectives. For example, when a customer receives bad work you tend to emphasize quality. When you're behind on shipments, you demand speed.

What you usually forget is to tell the employees in question that you have changed your tune, the reason for it, and how long the change is going to remain in effect. Most Businessowners have a consistency rating among employees a little below Jimmy Carter's.

Recognizing employees for doing good work is not idle flattery or mush-headed management, but silly compliments fall into that category. When your employees accidentally do something right — and sometimes you have to be very observant to catch them in the act — it doesn't cost a damn thing to tell them so.

Now what do I mean by respect? Don't talk down to employees. As long as you are referring to the work itself and not to them personally, they get the respect they need. For example, try this: "The easiest way to hold a hammer is like this." Not, "This is the way *you* should hold a hammer."

Getting back to recognition, it's amazing how many Businessowners who never received any when they were on the bench behave as rudely toward their employees as their employers did to them.

For instance, I once managed to convince a drugstore owner that it would be to his advantage to recognize good work on the part of any employee caught in the act. After a couple of days, he called up and said that the girl in charge of greeting cards had done a great job straightening them out after the Christmas rush, so he told her so.

And then he said, "Let me tell you this, old boy, I'll never do that again."

When I asked him why, he said that after he had told the young lady how well she had straightened out the cards, they both stood there staring at one another in total embarrassment.

He had never given an employee any recognition and she, obviously, had never received any from him or other employers and was totally unnerved by the experience. It hadn't occurred to him to acknowledge her good work and go on about his business. He was glued to the floor.

Now let's talk about people not knowing what's going on. Summarized by the comment that all consultants hear, "Nobody ever tells me anything around here."

Your employees don't want to know your innermost financial secrets, although those who are inclined to do so could probably make pretty shrewd guesses. They do want to know the likelihood of continued employment, whether orders, supplies, merchandise or whatever are coming in as scheduled, and whether business seems to be OK generally. Whether any changes are in store that would affect their jobs, such as increasing or decreasing production, space, or business activity in any way, shape or form. Nor do they want to know very much about it.

Just enough so they don't feel in the dark. Like sex education for children. You don't give a five-year-old medical school lectures on the human reproductive system. Put another way, if somebody wants to know what time it is, you don't have to explain how to build a clock.

What has all this to do with getting people to apply for work? It's similar to building business. I told you earlier that the way to increase sales volume is to take care of the business that you have. By the same token, to improve the quantity and quality of job applicants, do a better job of making the employees you have more profitable to you. More details in the next chapter. Can't completely separate techniques of hiring from those of handling the help. When employees are satisfied with their jobs, they make more money for you. So the way to hire help is continually to teach and re-teach the employees you have.

As a result, two things will happen. Fewer people quit, and more apply. Word gets around that yours is a good place to work. Not as fast as if it were a bad place to work, but still it will get around.

Now that you have mended your ways regarding the help you've already hired and you want to encourage still others to apply in addition to those who do so of their own free will and accord, what are the sources from which you recruit?

Other than random walk-ins — the general public — you will attract jobholders now working for customers, suppliers, and competitors. Also, friends of present employees.

There is nothing wrong with offering a customer or supplier's employee a job. It won't cost you a source of merchandise or material, or cost you any business. It's not an insult. Whether the individual joins your company or doesn't, your relationship with the other firm is strengthened. You've paid the other businessowner a compliment. Sometimes you might talk to the other owner in advance, depending on the situation, but don't be afraid to pirate. It's one of the best ways of finding proven employees.

This might be a good point to digress a moment and talk about filling supervisory jobs.

Hiring supervisory help is exactly the same as hiring any other kind of help. First, let's dispense with the notion of promotion from within. This is a time-honored procedure lacking any relevance to the real world.

Hiring or promoting from within is closely related to doing so by seniority, as required by many labor agreements. Don't blame the unions, however, because it was the Businessowners themselves who started to promote by seniority long before unions were thought of in their present industrial form.

There's no relationship, as you all know between length of service and ability to handle a supervisory job. If you have someone on the premises who wants that job, either because it represents a promotion or a change, interview him the same as you would an applicant from the outside, and compare the results of that interview with others that you conduct.

Nor does technical skill imply any particular supervisory ability. And, as we have said earlier, ignore the individual who asks for more responsibility in favor of one who assumes it without asking, or without having it given to him. Look for the fellow who just takes over.

In wartime, it's called a battlefield commission. Privates or non-com have taken over units when their officers were killed or put out of action, without having had the benefit of the Fort Benning course in how a Lieutenant's wife should present her calling card to the Colonel's wife on Saturday afternoon. Smoke one cigarette — tobacco — and leave unless requested to remain.

Before hiring anyone — cat-sitter, carpenter, or controller — redesign the job in practical terms as it should be done now. Don't be governed as you think it was done by the previous jobholder. Nor should you assume that the duties will remain the same. Instead of writing out one of those backward sounding job descriptions in overly objective terms, simply list, precisely, what the person will do all day when hired. Remember, you're looking at the situation now, not as you think it might have been. Work backwards to determine the skills, knowledge, and experience needed to do it. Then interview, as outlined earlier in this chapter.

By using these methods, you will hire the most profitable employees. And if you treat your present gang as I have suggested in this chapter and will lay out in detail in the next, you will have less hiring to do.

But remember — you are hiring help — not building men, or women, or contributing to the betterment of society or giving people an opportunity to express themselves or to actualize themselves, whatever the hell that means.

# CHAPTER TWELVE

# Handling the Help

Independent Businessowners are the natural prey of every uncredentialed consultant, underpaid professor of business administration, and unemployed corporate bureaucrat who claims to know all about motivating employees.

The inventory of unread books, articles, "special reports," weekly reminders, and cassettes on motivation found in the offices of Businessowners throughout the land—not to mention brochures promoting seminars on the subject that should be routinely transmitted from the mailman to your wastebasket —represent enough paper to reforest Europe.

Why?

Because all these scribblers and yappers have, without a deliberate conspiracy, elevated employee motivation to an absurd degree of complexity.

The costly consequences of this copycat collection of cuttings has been to convert an inherently simple subject to such an intricate maze that many businesses are now run for the benefit of their own personnel departments rather than to make money. That's even dumber than running the business for the benefit of the employees generally.

I will now eliminate this obfuscation for you permanently.

This chapter is the last thing you'll ever have to read about handling help — OK, motivating — if you have to be a long-hair about it. Thereafter, it will be unnecessary for you to spend any more time on such trivia than it takes to identify and toss it.

The business of getting employees to do their work resolves itself to a simple idea and two brief lists. A list of things not to do and one of things to do.

When you accept the simple idea and avoid doing the things in the first list, you will already be sufficiently ahead of competition as to out perform it to the extent that your profits depend upon employee performance. If, in addition to remembering to avoid the things in the first, you also do the things in the second list, you'll be so far ahead that competition will never catch up.

The simple idea:

Even if you inherited the business, at some time in your life you must have applied for a job. Hard to believe that the heir to any business that is still independently owned has had absolutely zero outside experience. A paper route, mowing a neighbor's lawn, or baby sitting when you were in school.

When you were hired, you intended to do a good job! That's a simple idea. You did not intend to goof off or do lousy work.

Strangely enough — although the longer you've owned a business the harder it will be to believe this — everybody you have hired intended to do a good job the day they came to work. Sure, we all make mistakes hiring. Bring on people who have too little or too much skill for the job, not physically up to it, or not put together too tightly. Still, you pride yourself on enough ability to judge your fellow man that you would not have hired anyone who intended to do a bad job upon showing up for work.

With this as a major premise, why are you so troubled with employee attitudes as to consider every half-baked, canned motivational or training program that comes down the pike? Why can any glib character with 10 percent more language ability than an army mule and 5 percent more nerve than a rabbit earn anything from a modest living to a substantial income as a purveyor of such services and materials?

The reason is that Businessowners have discouraged job holders. The fancy, seminar buzz word for this is demotivation.

The Businessowner who can avoid discouraging employees does not have to do anything else to motivate them, and will enjoy a substantial lead over competition.

Homework: Before reading further, make a list of procedures you follow to beat people down. Now compare it with my list of most generally used techniques for discouraging employees. If you've invented any I have not covered, I'll buy a drink whenever you catch up with me.

Here's my list:

— Violate the rules of ordinary courtesy. Never say please or thank you.
— Bawl people out in front of other employees.
— Exercise the God-given right of owners to be sarcastic at every possible opportunity.
— Ask insulting, demeaning, pejorative questions while wearing a self-satisfied smirk.
— Over-supervise. Tell them not only what to do, but how to take every little step. Leave no room for initiative.
— Give all choices of shifts, overtime, travel assignments, etc. to your favorite employees.
— Take employees to the nearest bar on Friday night and show them how a real he-man handles his liquor.
— Enjoy extra-curricular romance with female employees. When you get tired of one, move on to another. But let me know when you find a woman businessowner reversing the mistake. The women I know who own businesses are much too practical for such nonsense.

The above methods are guaranteed to discourage employees to the point where they will have thoroughly forgotten the good intentions they brought with them when they came to work.

Now that you've listed the things not to do—and the simple act of not doing them will automatically put you ahead of competition—what positive actions can you take in handling the help that will make money for you? Bearing in mind that the employees are there for the benefit of the business, and that the business is not there for the benefit of the employees.

More homework: This time, before reading further, make a list of the positive procedures you follow to be sure that your employees maintain the good intentions and enthusiasm they brought to the first day in your place. If they work, keep it up. You may also want to add my list, which will follow a couple of paragraphs down.

The basic fact is that everyone who works knows two things. Knows he needs a 10 percent raise, and also knows that he's going to work at the going rate. Most jobholders in independently owned businesses understand that the only source of their wages is the money you receive for goods or services. The significance of this fact is that non-financial rewards are all you have to offer.

Or, "Man does not live by bread alone."

You and your competitors are all going to pay about the same wages. Sure, now and then you hear that an outfit with an unusual incentive program pays janitors $30,000 a year, etc. These schemes flame across the sky like a meteor and burn out. They die because it was never the compensation formula itself that enabled the firm to pay high bonuses, but the peculiar, temporary leadership quality of a dramatic personality.

So what are some of the non-financial rewards you have to give—that cost you nothing?

—  Let people work in an atmosphere of approval. You convey this by your own manner, like saying good morning as if you meant it.

—  Give employees information as to how they are doing.

Tell them—good or bad—frequently. If you don't, instead of working they'll spend time figuring out what's in your mind as far as they're concerned.

— Ask employees questions. For several reasons. First, you learn things about your business. Even the lowest paid employee knows something about his job that you don't. You may find that he is doing something unnecessary, or not doing what is necessary. Second, the employee feels good and works better because you have given him this recognition.

— Having asked the question, listen to the answer. Seriously. Don't just stand there and pretend to listen. Listen with your eyes as well as with your ears. No form of recognition equals rapt attention. Then follow up with another question. To prove you were listening.

If you have not been doing this, take it easy at first because employees might be terrified when you start asking questions. Takes time for them to learn that all you are trying to do is get information.

— Give out information. In the business world, a secret is something known only to one person.

In auditing the management and operations of dozens of companies, I've found that one of the most frequently repeated statements made by employees is, "Nobody tells me anything." They'll do a better job if they know what's going on. You have few, if any secrets.

— Encourage employees to set their own goals. Production quotas. They're more apt to attain them that way.

— On those rare situations when you find an employee doing something right, tell him about it immediately. It's the greatest non-financial reward a Businessowner or boss can bestow. You can afford to be generous in praise and recognition. Don't save it for salary review time.

— Finally, fire the drones. Good workers don't like to see dopes protected. As I've said right along, since employees are your biggest expense, weed out the weakest. As owner, one of your quotas should be to fire the least productive 10 percent of your employees every year.

Spend 15 minutes every month reviewing these lists of things not to do and things to do, and you'll maintain basic control of the help.

There are other aspects of the situation you should keep in mind.

Businessowners who do all these things still find too much attention soaked up by so-called personnel matters. Absenteeism. Tardiness. Requests for time off. Accidents. Bad Work.

It is easy to forget that many problems surfacing as employee enigmas are really rooted in unprofitable operating procedures, physical conditions, irrational combinations of duties, or poorly maintained equipment.

Again, the old unstated assumption. In these instances, it's that the employee needs to be lectured, indoctrinated, warned, disciplined, praised or fired. Sometimes that's right. Especially fired. But, again quoting that great businessman George Gershwin, "It ain't necessarily so."

For example, in large offices and stores we occasionally find a personnel manager who has attended too many seminars, busily engaged in maintaining complicated cross-referenced records and disciplinary documents concerning absenteeism and tardiness.

The faster presence and punctuality deteriorate, the more furious become the posting from time cards to attendance ledgers and issuing of warning slips with copies to everyone this side of the White House.

Some personnel managers have been known to parlay this kind of situation into hiring enough more clerks and statisticians to justify raises for themselves, as in government practice. And enough numerical nonsense has been known to merit a Master's Degree at the nearest night school.

In these situations we frequently find the cause to be poor light, heat, ventilation or no place to park. More recently, while it's illegal, immoral, and perhaps even fattening to consider age, race or sex in personnel selection, Businessowners can get brownie points from bureaucrats for discriminating

against an otherwise productive employee who enjoys an occasional cigarette—or heaven's no!—cigar. It's OK to take the
day off because someone else is smoking. Tobacco.

In manufacturing, it's customary to blame poor quality
work on indifferent employees. Often justifiably. But have
you checked production and inspection tools, jigs, and fixtures
lately? And on a regular schedule? And do some of your
machine tools require a magician rather than a machinist to
hold tolerances?

Why are Businessowners particularly susceptible to penny-
wise, pound-foolish policies? Because all the powers of decision are in one person. Both the strength and the weakness of
an owner. Freedom to save a buck today must be balanced
with the discipline needed to make a buck tomorrow.

One of the weaknesses, to which I may already have alluded, is the illusion of loyalty, which results in the trap of reverse
loyalty. And what—with apologies to Shakespeare's heirs and
legatees—is loyalty, but a word?

And what—without apologies to Dun & Bradstreet—is the
most insidious cause of business failure, but reverse loyalty?

Appears in various guises.

"Ajax has been with me from the beginning, and he's loyal."

"He may not be keeping up with the parade technically, but
he's loyal."

So what? Did you undertake to support Ajax indefinitely,
regardless of his contribution? And what has he done for you
lately?

What do you mean by loyalty? Does Ajax work extra hours?
Take work home? Is not looking for another job? Doesn't offer
trade secrets to competitors? Are there any? If so, could he
possibly understand them? All because he loves you?

Without a precise definition of the term, exclude loyalty as a
factor in determining whom to fire and whom to promote.
More on the delicious subject of firing in the next chapter.

Conversely, do the foregoing quotes from real live Independent Businessowners mean that the true situation is that
owners are loyal to employees? Before you say, "That guy

would go to hell for me," ask yourself whether you're letting your business go to hell for him.

Is he working for less money than he says he could get elsewhere because he is loyal, or because he knows nobody else would be so foolish as to hire him at half the price?

Are the salaried people who worked during a strike loyal to you, and opposed to the union? If they don't like the union, maybe that's because it shaves their authority, not because they are concerned about your pocketbook. They have the best of both worlds. You'll raise them too, after the union members get theirs, and they'll know why they got it. Or would you rather not think about that?

Why assume that so-called management employees identify their personal interests with those of your business? Their allegiance is to their own bank accounts.

Let's suppose Ajax gives a day's work for a day's pay, and speaks only well of you.

Is that a reason to keep him if his laudable efforts and sterling character no longer makes money for you?

Businessowners think of the supervisory employees they work closely with — if not the entire crew — as "my men." "My people." "My guys." And without putting it in words, assume that this comradely feeling is reciprocated in the form of an undefined loyalty. Never is.

The trap this unrequited warm feeling leads Businessowners to is the inability to reduce the scope and size of the jobs of these employees when they cease to enlarge their skills.

The trap tightens around your foot when you acknowledge the fact that you have surrounded yourself with mental pygmies, and start to run your business out of deference to the limitations of employees. Your function is to assign work and check to ascertain whether it has been properly performed. If you've followed the steps outlined in the previous chapter and this one, instead of basing business decisions on personnel weaknesses, you replace unsatisfactory employees one or two at a time.

After you have inadvertently built an organization on personalities rather than things to be done, you usually can't break loose without a major housecleaning. Nothing wrong with that, but you must have replacements lined up.

In this respect, the employees — sometimes called corporate executives — who hold down fat salary positions in the huge companies that nobody really owns, are more practical than Independent Businessowners. These fellows know very well that their peers and subordinates are constantly looking for ways to slide a knife into their ribs, in order to get their jobs or the one above. Know they are in a free-for-all without rules.

The most universal example of organizing the job to suit the employee — applies to practically any type of business — is the office. The office manager usually is an outgrowth of the job of the bookkeeper who eventually became, or was replaced by an accountant. By default, he was, and is — "in charge of the office." As the business developed, there was more paper to process — payrolls, receivables, payables, reports to government, and maybe even to you. He hired help to perform these chores, then ignored it and buried himself in his ledgers.

All this poor fellow ever wanted to do was accounting, and it strains his brain to keep up with the small part of that trade that he needs to know. He had neither occasion nor desire to learn how to supervise.

The owner normally reacts by regarding his poorly managed office as as inescapable weakness of his loyal accountant, who has been with him through thick and thin, ad nauseam. Not so.

## WHAT TO DO:

Appoint a straw boss — working clerk — over the other employees, who reports to you for personnel matters and goes to the accountant only for any procedural information she needs. She, because nine times out of ten it will be a woman who has mastered payroll, or payables, for example, and is capable of learning the other procedures and controlling a small crew.

Although most management consultants claim expertise in

this area, my observation has been that CPA's who have audited many companies are usually in a better position to install or improve paper flow systems. In the final analysis, most of this work is created by government regulations on the one hand, and the most elementary of "generally accepted accounting procedures" on the other.

This idea applies to other situations.

For example, you have a Chief Engineer who comes up with good designs but can't organize a drafting room. Appoint a working lead draftsman to report to you, organizationally speaking. He gets technical information from the so-called Chief, who has no supervisory function.

You don't have to mold your business to the mental contours of a man who is technically competent but unwilling to manage subordinates doing routine work. You can profitably limit him to what he does well.

The owner's reverse loyalty to employees—this will be emphasized in Chapter XIII—stops him from cutting them back to where they really want to be, but were afraid to say so.

On the other hand, the men who survive in the cannibalistic environment of major corporate fishtanks have no such problem. They cut and slice in every direction—with relish!

Example from manufacturing: When operations were smaller, minor design changes were made informally in the shop. Now, with volume you need at least some rough similarity between the prints and the parts. Still, your Bull-of-the-Woods insists on murdering any hope for interchangeability. You, as owner, must insist that he either get up to date and go through engineering or he's through. No use reducing his authority in order to retain his mechanical savvy. That would destroy his self respect and therefore his usefulness.

Example from drug retailing: Older clerks still spend time helping customers. Historically this boosted sales. Now high costs force drug clerks to function like supermarket checkers. If the Store Manager can't change their ways as well as his, replace the whole crew.

Early on I told you about the Independent Businessowner (it

was actually Oscar) who turned down an offer because he felt that his key men would not survive in a large corporation. Now what? He can't run the show forever, and has no business family behind him.

ESOPS may be good business for lawyers, but in Oscar's case as in most, the employees have neither the dollars nor the sense to take over.

Oscar's chances of attaining trade mark immortality would have been far greater had he sold to someone able to keep the outfit afloat.

In the last chapter I warned against basing promotion on seniority. Another example of wrong-headed reverse loyalty is unwillingness to promote a younger man over the head of an older one. The owner who lacks the nerve to fire a disintegrating oldtimer salves his conscience by excluding him from a general raise. The time-server is thus further disheartened, so his negative comments tend to discourage other employees.

This is the basis for many forced retirements from firms upholstered with pensions. But don't let the fact that you have avoided that blubber prevent you from running a still tighter ship.

WHAT TO DO:

Measure performance against specifically expressed standards. Number of things done. Number of errors.

Don't be impressed by expressed fawning sentimentality. Be loyal to your bank account. To do this, recognize the difference between an investment and an expenditure.

I've already introduced the startling concept that you have no investment in your employees. Depreciation, yes; depreciated value, no.

Now that in this chapter we're finally emphasizing how to think about practical ways of handling the help, let's explore the investment-in-employees fallacy a little further.

The delusion that employees are assets is a trap Independent Businessowners construct for themselves with tiresome monotony. Employees can neither be sold nor hypothecated. And the insurance costs continually escalate.

Increased usefulness or greater skill sometime occurs, but less than proportionately to the associated higher wages and benefits.

Employees cannot "become" more valuable. There is never a market value increase of a previous purchase. The only thing that can happen is that you spend money hoping to make them more profitable to you.

Funds spent preparing employees to work better or faster are an expenditure. Information has been imparted to employees, they have it, and there is no way you can take it from them. Dollars down the drain.

Some owners claim that money spent teaching employees new techniques constitutes a further "investment." Nothing could be farther from the truth. At least half the time, it is really throwing good money after bad. You can't take back any marketable skills they may have acquired at your expense.

When the Businessowner thinks of employees as assets, he then proceeds to compound the error by reacting to their behaviour as if he owned them. This means double frustration when they fail to perform as expected.

Some academics to the contrary, you can't successfully manage employees by a system of punishment and rewards, as you would dogs and horses. Cats don't fall for such transparent tricks.

But you don't mean it that way? You mean as a group the employees are more difficult to replace than designs, tools, inventory, soft-ware, etc.?

In the sense of a permanent, 100 percent effective strike, or an epidemic that wipes out the entire crew at once, you may have a point. But how likely is that? In the next chapter, we'll talk a little more about weeding out deadwood.

Employees are expenses and nothing but expenses. Although the personnel "workers" in your business keep records for the government, the important entries are not made in that baby-sitting department, but by accountants, under various expense categories.

You spend money on wages and benefits, and in teaching employees, but in no way are these expenditures recoverable.

WHAT TO DO:
Check the employment market before spending more dollars trying to make silk purses out of sow's ears.

There are lots of people out there waiting for your call. I told you in Chapter XI how to make sure they rattle your cage. They have acquired skills at somebody else's expense, don't know how things have "always been done" in your shop, nor what is impossible. Neither are they members of your various political factions.

After you stop thinking of employees as assets — when you have emerged from the intellectual sauna in which you have been immersed by muddle-headed, self or university-appointed experts in business — you will be ready for the next stage of enlightenment.

That breakthrough is the recognition that all employees are temporary. There is no such thing as a permanent employee. Everybody eventually dies, quits, retires, or is fired. Not enough get fired. More coming on that in Chapter XIII.

This dazzling insight will also enable you to avoid expecting a return from employees that they cannot give. The expectation of such a return is as practical as expecting gratitude, which your total life experience tells you is ridiculous. Ask the Shah.

WHAT TO DO:
Wash the concept of "my people" out of your mind. Expect measurable or countable work from everyone. Figure to lose them all within five years, and govern yourself accordingly.

This means that as a Businessowner one of the various crafts you are mastering is that of teacher.

Owners do a great job of teaching production or clerical workers how to supervise others except when they forget that their example carries more weight than their sermons.

Supervisory training starts before you appoint a new foreman, office or branch manager. How you decide what the job requires and who to select governs the teaching program. That's why the canned, or cookie-cutter approach is absurd. Rests on the unstated assumption that all employees and situations are the same. Before starting to instruct, be sure you have re-defined the job and—yes, again—and that the candidate knows what he will have to do all day and how he will be judged.

Develop measurable standards, preferably with his participation. The more clearly a supervisor understands what is required of him and how he will be judged, the less time he will waste trying to find out. And he will treat his subordinates accordingly.

Teach him to assign work, instruct people how to do it, check the work and make corrections. Hard for a new boss to assign work instead of doing it.

Much so-called supervisory training, books, and seminars dwell on the current fad, or highly-promoted manual on popular psychology, omitting anything about getting the job done.

All based on philosophy ranging from Aristotle through Freud down to the latest hot stuff in the *Ladies' Home Journal* or *Business Week*. Never on hard experience.

Teaching how to supervise is a continuous on-the-job proposition. Can't be done across the desk, in a classroom or even in seances conducted by consultants as a method of advertising their scintillating personalities and blinding wisdom.

Your purpose is not to teach cute psychological tricks and key phrases, but to convey a clear understanding what a department has to get done in what time cycles. The new manager is then in a position to explain matters to his subordinates.

The central theme to weave all through your drill is that the employees—managers included—are there for the benefit of the employees. Jobholders dealt with thus honestly bring a more businesslike attitude to their jobs than those fed the "one big happy family" hypocrisy. Nobody buys that garbage.

Your general business philosophy is the next thing the new

supervisor has to understand. That is, are you trying to provide what the market will want next month, or what you think customers ought to have?

A few basics the new foreman must know: What every employee in his department must do every day; that those who report to him know exactly what they are supposed to do and how to do it; and how their work will be judged; that his own credibility from day one determines the effectiveness of his leadership; how to rate performance, not people; and that he is not the Chaplain.

How to teach him? Break the job down into its smallest elements. Ask the new boss to tell you the work he will assign to each man and when it should be completed. Let him practice giving instructions while you pretend to be the employee. Fancy lingo for this is role playing.

Back in the 30's when I was lucky enough to have a labor job in a foundry, one of the men on the swing shift—a recent immigrant—said of his foreman, "I go to hell for that Swede."

Funny thing is that the Swede too had only been in the United States five or six years. Obviously, he had not attended any University Extension courses or privately promoted expensive seminars. Also obviously, he knew his business and was the type of square-shooter that men would work for.

Leadership—the kind the Swede had—has been around a couple thousand years before the invention of video tape and supermarket psychoanalysis.

About a year ago, I was in a large Washington, D.C. consulting firm where a very capable secretary was to be promoted to Office Manager. Although I've been there many times, for the first time she offered to shake hands. Said she had to practice her assertive handshake. Seriously.

After congratulating her, I asked what she thought was the most important thing about the job of Office Manager.

She replied that it was to set a good example as to attendance and punctuality. Although I questioned her further, she never mentioned anything about getting the work done right and on time.

As Eddie Guest said, "Keep your eye upon the donut and not upon the hole."

Only you can teach your employees — mainly by example. And by the way, in case I didn't ask in Chapter IX, have you re-defined your own job lately, decided what to do to upgrade your own skills? Of course you have.

Organizing the work is half the battle of employee motivation. Efficiency is the result of doing only what is necessary. For that reason, highly touted schemes to achieve work simplification miss the mark. Your real objective is work elimination.

Whatever you're doing can be done with fewer employees. Most Businessowners recognize this fact from time to time and react by laying people off. Although this usually has a salubrious effect on those remaining, as well as temporarily reducing expenses, in the long run it's not the most effective procedure.

Work simplification is a good exercise for industrial engineers who assume things have to be done, and are skilled in finding simpler — and, give them credit — less costly ways of doing them.

Take painting, or other surface-treating, for example. The corporate nursemaid or his industrial engineer squeezes most waste motion out of the operation. On the other hand, the Businessowner looks for the reason to do the job in the first place. Many parts don't need it!

Warehousemen and stock room workers efficiently arrange boxes or trays of parts and finished goods. All 4" flanges or 6-oz bottles lined up together. Neatly. The owner should ascertain whether, by applying brains and memory, the material could be deployed equally well from wherever it landed, without all the efficient relocating and record-keeping.

Don't worry so much how efficiently your employees are working. Record every task performed, and ask for what purpose. There's a theory that an outside consultant can do this better because, not having seen the operations for years, he is more apt to notice things that you, the owner, have learned to take for granted.

Perhaps. If you do it first yourself, however, you'll pay the consultant for fewer hours. And as you eliminate work—jobs, employees, and their horrible costs melt away!

At this point in a session, a client often asks, "Is there some formula by which I can rate my employees?"

As is so often the case, this is the wrong question. Rate performance, not people. Be sure you know exactly what you want them to do and that they, in turn, understand your instructions. Sounds easier than it is.

One way to find out whether your instructions were understood is to ask the employee to play them back to you.

Some owners operate on the assumption that both they and their employees know what is to be done, and fear that they might look foolish if they delve into the matter.

Establish clearly in your own mind how you intend to judge performance—not people. Output. Accuracy.

Don't judge emotionally. That's judging people. Many Businessowners who put in countless hours are prejudiced against "key" (supervisory) employees who are not equally absorbed by their careers. Judge performance—results. What has actually been done? How well? Not how much time has been spent looking busy, or hanging around to impress you. Employees who are there all hours are not necessarily making you money.

Construct objective standards of measurement and ignore personalities.

Many more jobs than you would think lend themselves to measurement. In an office, for example, the number of pieces of paper processed and errors made—purchase orders, payables, receivables—can be counted.

In engineering departments of manufacturing operations, judge routine work by the number of dimensional changes legitimately requested by the production department.

(Chief Engineers avoid having their performance rated, by

cleverly outmaneuvering owners' efforts to define their jobs.)

Businessowners who have done this—taught themselves to judge the work rather than the worker—pride themselves on not having yes-men. Encouraging everyone to express their views.

The insidious trap they thereby set for themselves lies in the unstated assumption that men either yes you or stand tall only in debate. In reality, they mainly yes your personal idiosyncrasies.

Shows up most clearly when the troops know a promotion is up for grabs. Regardless of the enterprise.

For example, a manufacturer who operates machine shops in Los Angeles and Houston is a bear for neatness and orderliness. Convinced that these qualities have a direct bearing on profitability. Other things being equal, maybe so.

The L.A. operation is cleanest in the West. Eat off the floor. Pass a military white glove inspection. Houston, on the other hand, looks like any machine shop. Except that a firm of industrial engineers, after making adjustments for wage differentials, etc. found it to be 20 percent more efficient than L.A.

Yet, when the job of Vice President, Manufacturing, was created, the Los Angeles Manager got the nod. Had "presence," and other qualities described in the *Harvard Business Review*. The fellow in Houston merely made more money for the company.

Possible the California man really had more latent capacity, but henceforth those looking for promotion will sacrifice profitability on the altar of neatness.

Another fellow has built a nationwide representative organization selling several complicated, related lines of processing equipment. Prides himself on his excellent command of English. His precise letters and the quotations he writes are close to grammatical perfection.

His Midwest manager of fifteen years, Joe, has the best record in the company, with increasing volume every year. Although his quotations are understandable, his English is bad. Joe has also trained a number of men, who after getting their own territories still call upon him for help in preparing proposals. When the owner eventually recognized the need for a Sales Manager, however, Joe was passed over.

Perhaps the anointed one, who didn't sell as much, did have better qualifications, but Joe told others that the owner used to lecture him about his English. The word is out that to get favorable attention from the boss, you'd better be a good letter writer. Never mind the selling.

Both entrepreneurs boast they will not tolerate yes-men in their companies!

WHAT TO DO:

Clearly define the job and the qualifications necessary to get it. Decide how you are going to measure or rate candidates, how much weight will be assigned to track records, and how much to personal judgment. Let these things be known to all concerned.

Pay is at once the hardest and easiest problem to solve in handling help. Hardest because you have to get the money. Contrary to the affectations of journalists and popular psychologists, meeting a payroll is not a funny idea or expression.

Pay is the easiest problem to solve because your competitive situation determines the amount. And, as I've pointed out before, people who work for wages know that they are going to get the going rate in the industry, whether it is determined by collective bargaining in large companies, government subsidy, or the newest plant in Japan or Germany, which amounts to the same thing.

What every Businessowner wants most is employees, especially so-called management employees — an important-sounding word for straw bosses who have desks — who will demonstrate the same interest in the business that he does.

The ankle-crushing trap he usually stumbles into is an incentive plan. Profit-sharing. Bonuses by formula. Dividends on imaginary shares of stock.

The complexity of such schemes is limited only by the daydreams of the owners and the ingenuity of consultants who make their living by installing them in a manner that eventually causes so much confusion that their engagements are renewed three or four times to straighten things out.

By then everyone has forgotten that it was the original engineering of the compensation package that booby-trapped the outfit, with blame for the costly catastrophe assigned to its administration.

The unstated assumption on which these programs are promulgated is that the desire for gain is the only component of the owner's financial motivation, and therefore the transfer of this desire to employees will make them more productive.

Forget for the time being such non-financial stimuli as "winning the game," "sense of achievement," "self-actualization" — there's a great one! — and similar inanities attributed to us by perennial pupils called Professors of Business Administration.

The fallacy in the unstated assumption that gain is the owner's sole motivation lies in its failure to recognize that Businessowners are motivated as much by fear of financial failure as prospect of profits.

If you doubt that statement, ask yourself whether you sweat more pursuing a new order, or trying to round up the cash to meet your payroll (not on old joke) or your note at the bank?

If the worst happens, your overpaid and underworked employees will only miss an extra check already earmarked for unnecessary puchases, but you stand to lose your entire roll. And more.

Nor does the possibility of losing a job have the energizing effect on employees that the fear of ruin (an old-fashioned word) has on owners. Most people figure they can always get another job when unemployment insurance runs out, feel no disgrace in accepting it or even downright welfare when they are not looking for work, and no kick from conscience in postponing payment of bills indefinitely.

The main reason union members fight discharge is the pleasant anticipation of being re-instated by an Arbitrator — more on this in the next chapter — and getting paid for not working during the time they are off, plus the sheer joy of rubbing the boss's nose in the dirt.

Until there is a negative incentive — until employees have something real to lose — they will remain on the one-way street they've always been.

"What about the successful incentive plans?" you ask. "Those which have proven themselves?"

Compared to what? People who construct complicated compensation contrivances can always make a case to "prove" success. Simply because there is usually insufficient data available for accurate measurement of results.

Granting that a few have "worked," such as the formula invented by John C. Lincoln of Lincoln Electric Welding some years ago, and the wild Jack & Heintz deal of World War II fame, the truth is that these men were charismatic leaders who were successful before they designed their showy salary systems. They probably could have reached the same bottom line by paying 10 percent under the minimum wage.

It's now how much or what basis you pay the help that counts. It's how clearly you both know what's to be done, how skillfully duties are taught and work is corrected, how quickly workers are recognized when they occasionally do something right, and how believable you've been over the years that make the difference.

Independent Businessowners hire salesmen, retail clerks, or waiters. Eventually Sales Managers, Store Managers, or Head Waiters — on commission or bonus.

And are amazed when those so compensated sell like blazes with no thought for profitability. Why should they? You're not only paying them on total volume, but are operating on the unproven assumption that you need a full line which includes many low-profit or unprofitable items. The full line fallacy described earlier, also comes into place in connection with handling the help.

Makes no difference whether you are a manufacturer, wholesaler, distributor, retailer, restauranteur or other type of entertainer.

This particular trap — paying the same commission on non-profitable as on profitable sales—which seems to have a mysterious attraction for Businessowners, is called a consistent policy.

The most you can expect from a supervisory employee on an override is more business plus an instinct for following the path of least resistance in both sales and credit.

And before you criticize the Sales Manager for not looking beyond the end of his nose, remember that the minute he does so—starts fooling around with the long view—he has stopped selling and gone to philosophizing.

As owner, the job you delegate at greatest period is that of studying the market to find out what it will really pay for which goods or services, and writing the price list accordingly.

If your customers are other businessmen, the answer depends on how skillfully you establish that they can make more money buying from you than from your competitors. If your customers are consumers the answer depends on how well you satisfy their practical or emotional requirements. Needless to say, price is the last thing your customers will consider if you study their business or personal make-up.

WHAT TO DO:
Get out from behind that desk and go where the customers are, individually and in groups. If they are having a convention the only mistake you can make is to stay home. And don't forget that the financial cemeteries are filled with headstones of individuals who used to be Businessowners, but became executives who stopped making calls or greeting shoppers. Here is another illustration of the impracticality of separating the personnel and marketing functions of a Businessowner. Admittedly, conventional business books insist on doing so, and I expect the horrified disapproval of doctoral candidates in the field.

Establish a sliding scale of commission or bonus rates, so that the least profitable sales yield the lowest rewards. The bookkeeping isn't that hard!

There are many types of incentive schemes. Each Businessowner must find the one that best suits his business, his personality, and the way he supervises those who work for him.

The value of any incentive method depends upon how consistently employees are reminded of their benefits under it. It's generally more effective to do this with Sales and Marketing types than with Manufacturing and Production workers. The more complicated—and larger—the manufacturing operation, the more difficult to make money with incentive systems. Too much bookkeeping. Too many explanations. Just plain too complicated.

Salesmen, of course, are usually paid at least partly on an incentive basis, but not enough other people who help bring in business get their share of this extra pay.

This is especially true of Marketing people—including promotion and advertising—whose efforts are hard to relate to specific incoming business. On the other hand, they have a great deal to do with creating sales volume. Their contribution must be recognized in some tangible way if you want them to keep it up.

We know of one organization that has been successful paying cash bonuses to the entire Marketing group, based upon increased business over similar periods in previous years. Again, however, each program has to be designed for its particular situation.

The creative staff in the back room bear the same relationship to salesmen as the artillery and air force do to the infantry. It's hell to advance without cover!

Don't worry about setting precedents. In fact, it's a good idea to establish the precedent that people who produce more get paid more. Because you have one employee on incentive does not mean that you must put others on it.

Another area of confusion concerns the effect of a Union Agreement on the unorganized help.

Following a battle, the union gets a raise. If not a union in your plant, in the one that sets the pace in your area.

You then wait a while as if that fools anyone, and give roughly similar increases to clerks, typists, etc.

To compound the delusion you wait a little longer to pass it along to higher paid supervisors and other so-called "management" people.

Some larger companies attempt to conceal the fact that the raises were given because the union got one, behind the facade of a "salary review," to be followed in most cases by a "merit increase."

The salary reviews may not occur for several months after the new rates go into effect, but by varying their timing, "management" expects the resulting increases to appear somehow unrelated to the amount the union received.

Many of you give cost-of-living increases by formula to all employees. In this case, too, the non-union employees know perfectly well that their cost-of-living benefit was created by your union or organized labor in general.

There are a number of things wrong with this system. First, it is hypocritical. Employees know it, and this makes them less likely to believe an owner when he tells the truth about something else. They have heard him lie about their more important concern.

Another ridiculous consequence of this charade is that it destroys the validity of a merit increase that is truly earned.

WHAT TO DO:

First, be truthful with employees. A luxury available to Independent Businessowners, but not so often to the higher paid employees of large corporations. In order to maintain their "management position," they lie to those beneath them. This is another instance in which Independent Businessowners should not blindly imitate the administrators of firms nobody really owns.

Next, recognize that there is a general wage level you can do nothing about. When you find the rare employee who really does more or better work than others, pay him more. Who among you have not paid a union man above scale?

Then why not acknowledge to non-union employees that you're going to pass on the increase to them that you permitted the union to beat out of you? And state that anyone who deserves a merit increase will get it.

Such raises might be strictly discretionary, or you may enjoy fooling around with rating scales, patterned interviews, avuncular sessions which usually cause employees much private mirth, or even goal-in-life scenarios. These are an absolute riot.

You might say that if you acknowledge to non-union people that you're passing on to them the raise that was beat out of you by the union, that this will cause them to join the union. Not so. The information available as to why people join unions usually points more to grievances — and not many of them financial, at that — than to the satisfaction of getting a raise.

As a Businessowner you may think that people who work for a living are not very bright, but they know which side of their bread is buttered. The fact they make poor political decisions and are sold all manner of ridiculous products by TV, does not mean they are completely oblivious to their own financial welfare.

It's only a few Independent Businessowners and most of the supervisory employees of large corporations who make business decisions for reasons of pride or politics. Working people don't have to do this.

Another misnomer that unnecessarily beclouds the issue is the word "salary" as applied to the compensation of people subject to the Fair Labor Standards Act. If employees are covered by the Act, what benefit is there to the fiction that they are "salaried?" It just means extra bookkeeping. The "salary" has to be divided by 40 to get an hourly rate. They are wage earners. Respect them as such.

Possibly this is a carry-over from the days when salaried people enjoyed sick-leave, paid holidays, vacations, group insurance, and pensions, which were then not available to hourly rated employees.

Today the reverse is often true. Union workers frequently have better benefits than the white-collar crew. In fact, after submitting to some outrageous demands, many Businessowners have found ways to include key men and actually participate in such "fringes" personally!

In sum, why not be honest about the deal?

Now let's look at your Sales Manager. Is he making more than you are? Or, do you just think he is? Or, is it such a bad idea?

What does he do all day? Manage sales or keep track of them? Negotiate with production for better shipping promises? Settle commission disputes?

Or, does he work with his men to set objectives by product lines, lines of trade and territories within measured periods? Write snappier literature? Hold practice selling sessions with seniors as well as juniors? Seniors sometimes need it more by virtue of maintaining the same accounts for years.

Does he know as much about the world you are selling to and its people, as anybody in that field? Does he use this data to make money for your company?

Is he studying the economics of your customers' industry as well as your own? And does he know what competition is really doing, not just what a few imaginative salesmen say is going on?

In short, is he following or leading his men?

Two kinds of sales manager traps await the Independent Businessowner, both of his own making:

First trap: To avoid a high fixed commitment you put your sales manager on a total override, with no house accounts. Then, through such windfalls as unexpected government orders, or federal regulations mandating that all machine shops buy four of your widgets for safety reasons, you find yourself paying a ridiculous amount for a clerical function.

WHAT TO DO:
Either live with the situation, or if you take that class of business away from the sales manager, give him a higher rate on the business he gets, or change the salary-incentive ratio. Ride it out for the year. Change in the middle of the period and you lose credibility.

If the Sales Manager, or a salesman hits an unearned bonanza for any reason during the year, pay it gracefully and secure your reputation for keeping your word. Renegotiate, if necessary, the following year.

But if he strikes gold as a result of his efforts, you want him to benefit accordingly, and be motivated to sell still more.

An owner who draws less regular compensation than he pays his Sales Manager has decided to leave money in the business either for expansion or to boost the eventual sale price of the company. Fine, as long as the IRS doesn't assess it as undistributed profits. You must remind yourself of that deliberate decision when comparing your draw with the Sales Manager's.

A sub-trap is making a deal with your Sales Manager without a time limit. All compensation should be fixed for a set period, usually one year, unless your industry needs a longer cycle. If heavy pioneering is required, make the initial agreement for a longer period.

Second trap: Greed. Also of the owner's making. Investment counselors, whose advice is usually less profitable than the proverbial dart board, are fond of warning against decisions based on fear and greed — as if any other motives were available in commerce.

Properly used, both fear and greed are healthy emotions, necessary to self preservation. Greed becomes a trap, however, when employed without consideration of consequences.

If you appoint a Sales Manager, and he sells your widgets at profitable prices with an eye to future business, and at the same time you choose to invest the profits in your company rather than pay yourself, be happy the fellow is getting rich. Brag on him. Tell the world you pay your Sales Manager more than you pay yourself. Your peers will merely smile knowingly.

Don't let competition steal your man.

About ultimatums. Independent Businessowners who start figuring furiously when they get a "Pay me more or I'll quit" demand from a seemingly ace salesman will be pushed around by other employees.

Those who say, "See Joe in accounting for your final check" are in control of their affairs.

While there may be occasions when you should try to hold on to the fellow, any instant reaction that you must is based on at least eight unstated assumptions and one dereliction of duty on the part of the owner. The assumptions are that:

1.    He is worth a special effort to keep. Really is responsible for all those orders coming in from his territory. How much is new business? How much repeat? How tough is competition? Any chance he is getting business by default? Does the particular product mix going into the territory enjoy favorable production, quality control, and delivery status in your plant, store or warehouse? Does he get more special help from you or other technical experts in the outfit? In brief, is he as hot as he seems?

2.    He is not bluffing. Amazing how frequently employees fabricate offers of better paying jobs. How to find out? Say that you don't expect him necessarily to identify the other company, but keep him talking about the nature of the opportunity, compensation, etc. Listen for contradictions.

3.    He is not kidding himself. Also startling how frequently employees hear only what they want to hear when somebody is propositioning them. Does he know all the details of the job? How long others have lasted? How dependable are their quality control, service, and shipping promises?

4.    You "can't" pay him more. Why not? Have you calculated the true break-even point in this case? Salaries and commissions in the owner-run business are seldom governed by ability to pay. A matter of willingness to pay. It's your money. But don't muddle your thinking with unsubstantiated notions of "industry practice," or false constraints based on what you are paying others. Make a specific business decision for a business reason. Don't get tangled up in your own policy. You're not the prissy personnel manager of a private-sector political fishpond.

5.    You can make a deal with him that will stay put for at least a year. Sometimes self-intoxication sets in when an individual has enjoyed success, and you can't live with him no matter what you do.

6.    You have been giving him enough praise and recognition. Psychological rewards again. Sounds nuts, but Napoleon

said that, "A man will walk through the gates of hell for a piece of ribbon to pin on his tunic."

7.   Money is his real reason for getting out. Maybe he just can't stand working for you any longer.

8.   You can't replace him with a better man for less cost.

Which leads to the dereliction of duty on the part of the owner I alluded to before listing the foregoing assumptions. The duty of killing all your employees on paper — preferably one at a time — and keeping active files on replacements available both within and outside of your company. Checking competition. Suppliers. Customers. Vendors of related goods. That's another definition of "knowing the territory."

Handling the help is as simple as making babies. Both activities have suffered from too much philosophizing — or downright yapping — by academics who have had insufficient practical experience.

# CHAPTER THIRTEEN

# Firing the Help

Is there a single weakness shared by all Independent Businessowners? Regardless of whether you own a factory, retail store, restaurant, warehouse, industrial distributorship, or fleet of trucks?

And if there is, how does it relate to the economic pickle our politicians have put us in, and what should you do about it?

Since you've stayed with me this far, you know that Businessowners are capable of basing decisions on countless unstated, invalid assumptions; illusions and delusions; and that owners make mistakes of omission and commision every day, yet survive because of their energy, instincts, and judgment.

No individual owner has inflicted all or even the majority of the wounds I have described on himself. Obviously anyone who did so would long since have been entered in Dun & Bradstreet's annual necrology.

Still, there is one weakness that every Businessowner has. It is keeping employees he knows should be fired.

Show me the Businessowner who complains about labor turnover and I'll show you one who hasn't fired anybody in years. The turnover is entirely people who quit of their own

223

accord because the owner did not follow the methods of selecting and handling the help I have outlined.

Why don't you fire people? Favorite excuse is you don't have anyone at hand to replace them, so you retain unprofitable employees.

Real reasons are probably laziness, inertia, and the reverse loyalty to which I have alluded many times, which probably has done more damage to independently held businesses than any other single factor.

It's the business equivalent of leukemia. Slow death by barely perceptible stages in the beginning. Eventually it goes hard and fast and there's nothing you can do about it.

We've been propagandized by the same forces that have convinced jobholders that owners are inherently mean, and somehow don't have the right to own their businesses. In movies, television, etc., the Businessowner is the villain. There is a school of thought that attributes this to a communist plot.

The simple truth is that there are more wage earners than Businessowners. Owners normally get more money than their employees, who are jealous. It's only human for the latter to attribute the disparity to the idea that the former must have stolen the business or is in some way evil, because the alternative—that the owner has worked harder or is smarter than they are—is too hard to accept.

Chances are that communist film writers might have piggybacked on this idea and turned it to their advantage the way the Russians turn every kind of bad situation in the world to their advantage, and thereby got credit for starting fires that they merely fanned.

The disparity between boss and worker, master and serf, overlord and vassal, etc. is nothing new in the world, and existed long before communism was invented.

So much for theoretical background.

Businessowners are normally quick to fire for behaviour which usually results in arrest. Theft. Embezzlement. Arson. Assault and battery.

But not quick enough to fire for unsatisfactory output. Yet

you know that not all employees are equally profitable. Worse, you know some are marginal, and a few are a downright loss. But for reasons outlined above, you haven't fired them.

Since most owners have been following reasonably conservative financial policies, firing employees now becomes the most immediate way to rein in costs.

Note that I didn't say lay people off, or reduce the force. I'm assuming you need the help, and urge that you upgrade it to meet hard economic conditions. Remember, your competition is not limited to others in your field, but includes everyone who sells anything to your customers. That's the link between the importance of firing the least productive employees, and your marketing and profit plans.

Another reason you don't fire more people has to do with the presence of a collective bargaining agreement, or fear that employees might organize if anyone were fired.

This concern with union matters permeates your thinking not only regarding blue collar employees, but also the white collar group, traditionally unlikely to join unions. Finally, it's not pleasant to fire people. But you have to do a lot of things you don't like to do.

Let's clear away some underbrush on this matter of firing union members.

Although details vary somewhat according to the way a Labor Agreement is written, generally when grounds for discharge have been established, the employee should receive an oral warning in the form of an attempt to help him improve his work.

If he does not improve then he should receive one or two written warnings with copies to the union, and if after this the work is still unsatisfactory, fire the person.

Before doing so, be sure your case is in order and ask yourself how you would judge if you were an impartial arbitrator.

Independent Businessowners who fire union members without going through a series of warnings, invite an Arbitrator to force them to rehire such employees with full back pay and all benefits. Lose money and lose face.

But is it always entirely bad to lose a case and suffer such consequences? Strangely enough, the answer is not necessarily. Aside from the tiresome moral sentiment that we learn from adversity, losing a case can teach practical lessons.

You learn what you did wrong before you fired the individual, and what you did wrong in presenting your case to the Arbitrator.

In case the dust jacket of this book does not mention it, I've earned the right to talk about this in three ways. First, when I was in business my plants were organized by four unions on the West Coast and one in the New York area. We won grievances before Arbitrators simply by doing our homework. One in particular had the reputation of hoping the union would win, but he is a good lawyer and a fair Arbitrator. He castigated me thoroughly, but we won cases. Also, in those dread days beyond recall, I was President of an employer's union that negotiated many agreements in the San Francisco Bay area.

Second, I've coached Businessowners in labor relations for years, and third — and this is the dreadful thing that may have been delicately eliminated from the dust jacket — I have functioned a number of times as an impartial Arbitrator in labor-management disputes, including discharge cases. Yes, the unions know that I am both actually and philosophically a capitalist, but accept me anyway. You probably didn't know I was such a square shooter.

It's fine to hire an expert labor lawyer to represent you in a discharge grievance, but he is at a serious disadvantage unless he was involved in your negotiations and/or has a working knowledge of how things are done on your floor. Otherwise, you're well advised to be represented by your principal spokesman during negotiations and/or by your plant or store manager, possibly backed up by an attorney.

Regardless of the professional expertise you hire from the

outside, or the nature of the working relationship between your supervisory employees and the local union leadership, prosecuting a discharge before an Arbitrator is a special situation, and requires people who have a feel for it.

This book is not the place to go into the nitty gritty of preparing for an arbitration, but the points I am making will help you get over your reluctance to fire your least productive employees, even if such action may result in union grievances.

Consultants are often asked, "How can I fire a union man?"

Wrong question. What you really want to know is how to fire him so he will stay fired.

This implies, as we've been saying, a labor agreement with a grievance procedure ending in arbitration. In a discharge arbitration, the employer's representative must function as a prosecuting attorney. You have to prove you had just cause. This means you can't fire a man because of his union activities, or because he gives you a pain.

He must have done something for which he could be arrested, or violated posted rules, or failed to perform on the job in the same manner as other employees you are not firing. You have to prove he did not do the same quality and quantity of work as others.

Without good records to substantiate this, you will have difficulty making your discharge stick. Your foreman's, or your own judgment, is not enough.

If you don't have the necessary attendance, production, and quality control records, it would be sound business to maintain them quite apart from the matter of discharge.

To return to the hidden benefits of losing discharge cases, you learn not only how better to handle disciplinary procedures in the shop, but how to improve the overall supervisory techniques used by you as well as by your supervisory employees who supposedly represent you to subordinate employees.

Further, when an Arbitrator rules against you, in effect he tells you what you would have had to do to win. Therefore, the employee in question is also on notice as to what he has to do to avoid being fired a second time. So, if the situation is repeated, you will be in good shape to win.

You thereby not only improve your chances in future arbitrations, but may salvage an employee on whom you have spent considerable money.

Finally, all your employees, including the supervisory staff, as well as the union leadership knows that you are going to assert your rights under the agreement, and that you won't be a pushover every time the union is forced to grieve.

Arbitrations are expensive to labor organizations as well as to business, and labor officials prefer to avoid them to the greatest extent possible. Sometimes, of course, they are politically forced to process weak cases, but that's their problem.

If there is a single admonition to Businessowners or those who represent them in such matters, it is to be sure that all employees in the group are treated equally with respect to what is required of them and in disciplinary measures handed out. The easiest and most effective way for a union to win a discharge arbitration is to show that the employer has been applying discipline unevenly among the various members of the union, or for that matter among employees not in the union.

Disciplinary procedures applied to supervisory or professional employees is a totally different matter.

Businessowners who give even one warning as such to a truly supervisory employee have earned in full measure the embezzlement, sabotage, sale of trade secrets and loss of productivity they get. Lose money and more money.

Don't warn real supervisors or other non-union, salaried employees. Just fire them.

You might say that if you treat supervisory and similar salaried employees in this manner that you are pushing them into unions. Only true to the extent this group — small department heads, etc. — would have felt the need for union protection for other reasons.

In large factories where foremen are unionized they are

treated the same as other union members. Again, they are working foremen or the equivalent. No one pretends they represent the interests of the owners. And it's hard to believe that automobiles, for example, would be any cheaper if this group were not organized.

We are concerned here, however, with Independent Businessowners who do not have vast numbers of supervisory employees to tempt union. Possibly a superintendent and half a dozen foremen, plus the usual component of pencil-pushing supernumeraries.

Most line supervisors or sub-department heads are no different from other employees, except that they supply limited instruction and guidance to machine tenders, clerks, drivers, cooks, etc. No sure power to hire and fire.

When this intermediate bunch is unorganized, it is usually because of a collective bargaining process in which the union has extracted higher wages in return for leaving some people out of the union who would otherwise have been in.

In most cases, their supervisory role would collapse under a wage-hour audit, and the union has simply out-maneuvered an owner who places a greater value on the illusion that his first level straw bosses and office staff are "my guys" and are on "my side," rather than on the same "side" as the organized clerks, waiters, machine tenders, etc.

On the other hand, the minute you have issued a warning to someone who has responsibility, who acting on his own judgment spends your money — bona fide Superintendent, Controller, Purchasing Agent, Design Engineer, etc. — you have alienated him.

He can no longer even pretend to be "on your side" to any degree at all. He may never have been to the extent that you told yourself he was, but now he is completely an embittered, working stiff in every sense of the word, and feels the normal resentment. Very few Businessowners can convince such an individual that an actual warning is justified.

Since even when dealing with union members, a warning without instructions as to how to improve the work and thereby purge the record is meaningless, obviously when a non-union employee falls down on the job, it's up to you to ascertain why and help him discover what to do to improve his work. But don't warn him directly!

Laying out the necessary corrective action to be taken constitutes the warning, in fact, without destroying his self-respect and making an enemy of him.

What to look for? Health. Aches. Pains. Alcohol or other drugs. Whether he clearly understands what is required of him, and what standards you use to judge his work.

Frequently, for example, you change your thinking but neglect to explain the change completely to supervisory employees who report directly to you. Causes confusion. Or, supervisory work is getting to be too much for a man, he really would prefer to be back to the bench or the floor or whatever, but doesn't want to say so.

Since a demoted employee normally is useless, if you can't straighten him out without alienating him, your only alternative is to fire him. And in doing so, recapitulate your previous session in such a way that it is obvious that for practical purposes he has been warned and offered assistance.

While all this applies generally throughout the business world, one group merits special emphasis. Chief Engineers.

Chief Engineers don't get fired often enough. The client who reminded me of that used to be one, so he ought to know. Now that he's a Businessowner, he really knows.

Nor do equivalent top technicians, chemists, pharmacists, computer lunatics, or biologists. Especially when the owner is not personally expert in the field.

The trap Businessowners who didn't used to be technicians fall into is the unstated assumption that that class of help is so smart they don't need to be told, or at least not very often.

The trap unsupervised Chief Engineers, etc. fall into is the unstated assumption that everything will always go smoothly, and there is no reason to organize their departments to be ready for emergencies. That, plus an occupational inability to learn from experience.

And if you're a retailer facing irate customers, a dealer who didn't get delivery in time for your annual show, or a restaurant owner or food processor saddled with the creations of designers who failed to consider consequences, stick around. Insight into factory politics might give you an idea or two.

Here are two typical Chief Engineer evasions, with recommendations for the owner:

1. "We are too rushed. Didn't have time for extensive field testing."

"We" refers to his department, not the company. Responsibility is spread over subordinates. Chief Engineers act as if accepting personal responsibility is ground for being drummed out of the trade. The owner's job is to teach the Chief Engineer to accept responsibility for the work of his department. How many times have you repeated that lesson?

The other things he must be taught are how to supervise help to get things done on time, how to determine in advance if deadlines will be missed unless the staff is beefed up, and how to prepare for unforeseen calamities.

And about "extensive field testing." Have you hard evidence that experimental shop models being baby-sat by carefully selected and well entertained customers tell you anything about the dependability of subsequent run-of-the-mill manufactured products? Also, please let me know right away when you find the engineer who doesn't cheat just a little with those special darlings made by craftsmen. Just a tiny bit of filing here and there . . .

2. "We couldn't finish the new job because we were too busy putting out brush fires."

Who started the blazes?

There was only two possible arsonists. Either the widget wasn't designed right or it wasn't made right. If the prints are right and the parts are at least a little bit like the prints, no fire.

In the former case, you're back full circle to engineering incompetence, and in the latter you have a different but known candidate for decapitation. Manufacturing and production have to take turns pulling each other's chestnuts out of the fire, and it's the owner's duty to organize these efforts.

WHAT TO DO:

1.   Treat Chief Engineers the same as other employees.

2.   Be sure you know what you want them to do.

3.   Be sure they know it too, and how their work will be judged.

4.   When they blame others — manufacturing, sales, service, the Russians — for problems, question them about their own work.

And what happens when you do fire that prima donna?

A few months ago, a client called me and said, "I took your suggestion and fired the Chief Engineer. Now I run the thing myself — probably always did in reality — and have the crew supervised by the head draftsman. He doesn't think up anything new, but he doesn't have to. He does a good job of parcelling out the work and supervising five draftsmen and a clerk, but he goes into a state of shock when I come in and ask a question. He'll say anything that pops into his mind. How can I get him to calm down and give me a reasonable answer, or if he doesn't know it, simply to say so and tell me he will get back to me?

The answer, as it is so often, is to review fundamentals. The fundamentals of your job, not the other fellow's.

Back to square one in selling, seduction, and supervision. Instead of asking a closing question right off the bat, spend a few minutes listening to the poor fellow before getting around to what you really want to know. If possible, get him to talk first about something he has full command of. And sit down. Don't tower over him. Be sure you are following all the recommendations in this book concerning things to do and things not to do in hiring and handling the help.

In connection with this firing function of the Business-owner, the most irrational question I've ever been asked is, "What do you do about the marginal employee?"

The reply was simply, "Fire him." But that answer is apparently not satisfactory to everyone who asks.

The question is heard more often in large companies than in private businesses. Although you might not expect the question to occur to a Businessowner because he should know whether an employee's work is satisfactory, some owners have an unfortunate tendency to emulate the "management methods" of a golfing buddy who is Vice-President in charge of loose threads at a ribbon factory, or who is charged by a bank to decide whether to purchase round or square wastebaskets. So let's dig deeper.

Its origin lies again in judging people rather than work. Usually by using rating scales. Most such devices are concocted in large corporations, by college professors whose sole non-academic experience is summertime employment in such institutions, or by temporary help agencies calling themselves consulting firms who perform such advanced tasks and also serve as blame-takers for the private sector bureaucrats who staff these low-profit enterprises.

Most of them recoil from the prospect of a yes/no decision with a terror that should normally be reserved for meeting a coiled rattlesnake in the bedroom.

Accordingly, the rating scales they use — and you shouldn't — will include such checkpoints as "needs help," or "not up to potential."

This serves several purposes. Eliminates the hard work involved and responsibility for firing, and provides employment for the personnel or counseling department. Remember, life in a large corporation is a political career in which survival, much less advancement, depends on trading favors.

WHAT TO DO:

Back to fundamentals. To the lists of things to do, and not to do.

These fundamentals are dull and boring. They are neither exciting, nor creative nor challenging things to do. But remember in school the coach drilled you in fundamentals? In boxing, for example, the most important thing was to keep your chin down. The only reason anybody gets knocked out is that he ignores this fundamental and sticks his chin up in the air. Happens in business too!

By definition, Businessowners have employees. So some—maybe too much—of your time goes to your role as employer, instead of financier, producer, and marketer.

To reduce the time you play employer, drill yourselves on the fundamentals with respect to employees. Regularly. Just like the army puts units through basic training from time to time. Do this preventive maintenance consistently and you will have satisfactory employees. You won't have marginal employees because unsatisfactory people will have been fired or quit when it became clear they could not do the job.

Again, there are no marginal employees. Only marginal employers.

WHAT TO DO:

1.    List all employees in order of profitability to you. Do it objectively, based on practical work measurement.

2.    Tell those not doing what they should what is expected of them. Be generous in teaching and helping.

3.    If they can't or don't do it, after two warnings, fire them. Includes so-called supervisory and professional people, legitimately excluded from provisions of the Wage-Hour Act. This will have a beneficial effect on the morale of those employees you retain. Hard workers don't like to support drones.

To do this right means applying energy, attention, and dollars to the continuous improvement of techniques for the measurement of work and results.

You'll get further benefit—more money in your pocket—from this effort because it will automatically improve the overall efficiency of your business. Force you to find functions that can be eliminated. The crew will do a better job by virtue of knowing what you expect of them and how their work will be judged. So you won't have the unpleasant task of firing so many delightful people.

Until you have achieved this level of managerial supremacy, however, consider it a poor month in which you haven't fired the least profitable five percent of your employees.

# CHAPTER FOURTEEN

# Your Son, Your Son

"You're a lucky boy. I am lucky too. Why should there be two happy as we?"

Those words were sung by the ingenue to her beloved in the old musical, *Showboat*.

But have you, in effect, sung them to your son, as if the two of you were doing a soft shoe dance with straw hats and canes? And did you both long for it to be true while harboring doubts?

Don't skip this chapter if you are not burdened with an immediate descendant you "brought into the business." Because Businessowners in your situation are dangerously apt to anoint a younger, supervisory employee with substitute son status. Accordingly, much of what follows will apply to your attitude toward him and vice versa.

You've probably noticed that along with other areas of business management the shrinks, sociologists, and sob sisters have invaded the family business market to the extent there is now a mini-boom in the father-son relationship racket. The following thoughts and a few in the next and wind-up chapter

237

are the last things you'll ever need to read on the subject. True whether you are parent, child, or surrogate.

At the 1949 Tulsa oil show, half a dozen of us tending booths discovered we were all second generation in our firms. This led to the expression "SOB's" for "Sons of Bosses." Because of its obvious connotations, probably the expression is reinvented from time to time. It is my understanding now that an actual so-named organization exists someplace in the country. They have meetings, hear lectures, and "let it all hang out." Some such gatherings allegedly occur at resorts, golf clubs, and ships at sea. Maybe even on an occasional 747.

It's a real business. Apparently a travel agency entrepreneuer conceived the idea of a cruise consisting entirely of people who own family businesses. This is a unique development in the special tour game which had previously only subdivided its market down to conducting such conventional groups as left-handed chess players to Mongolia and nearsighted seamstresses to Perth Amboy.

Those tours or cruises are a great way to write off a family vacation. After all, wives are important in family controlled businesses and often are officers and directors of the corporation.

The program is based on the unstated assumption that mass psychotherapy can aid in the transmission of authority of father to son. Probably can't do any harm, but misses the point.

While all these activities undoubtedly make money for the tour directors, consultants, and professors involved, you are still stuck with the problem of letting Junior swipe your job.

In these situations, the son must be the aggressor. While there might be exceptions, the general rule is that if he doesn't grab the ball and run with it, the old man is not going to toss it to him. So, when an SOB complains to me that the old man won't give him authority, my answer is that it's your own fault.

In the last chapter, I reminded you how movies and TV had not been kind to Businessowners. Compared to the way they have treated sons of Businessowners, however, they practically venerate the older generation. The boss's son is traditionally portrayed as a punk, a dope, a lazy bum, or possibly all three. And, of course, some are.

Junior's real problem is that just as Businessowners half believe the movie versions of them, bosses' sons have in many cases bought the idea that there is something inherently bad about the opportunity to start near the top, and that the principle of inheriting anything—much less a business—is downright morally wrong.

Accordingly, to create the illusion that Junior too has "come up the hard way," Businessowners have been given the silly advice to treat their sons like any other employee. Since he's not the same as any other employee, it's ridiculous to pretend he is. Who is deceived? For what purpose?

Where this is the situation and the son is assigned to a dopey job, he simply has to do the same thing that any other aggressive employee would do, which is grab responsibility which he has not been given.

To him I say, as soon as you learn an operation, steal control of it. Don't wait for the set up man to hand you the next job, or ask the Controller whether you should move on to the general ledger, or the Sales Manager what territory you should goose.

Of course you'll make mistakes. But while there are many causes for which the old man might fire you, rest assured that one is not for doing more than you are asked to do. If you find this too difficult for your delicate nature, quit, get a job elsewhere if you can, and find out what life is really like.

One of the easiest ways to get responsibility and pull authority from it without having it conferred upon you, is to answer employees' questions—assuming you have any reasonable notion of what the right answer should be.

Regarding relationships with employees, again there is no use pretending to be one of the gang. They behave differently around you, and control what they say when within your hearing.

Some will try to use you as a means of advancing their own

careers, especially by cutting down rivals. In many firms, employees work assiduously to involve the boss's son in their own political schemes. The smart way to deflect such monkey plans is to avoid discussing any employee with any other employee — especially department heads. Be particularly suspicious when they say something complimentary about the other fellow. It's a trap. Shut up. Change the subject.

In most cases, it's easier to let your son steal authority from you than it is to give it to him. If he's stolen it fair and square, it's more truly his, and he can use it more successfully.

How? Some day he'll be on the premises when you're not. Maybe you're fishing or just spending the afternoon in a bar. A crisis will occur. A department head — one of "your guys" — will rush up to Junior and demand to know how to find you. Junior doesn't know, or pretends not to, makes the decision and tells the supervisory employee what to do. If he's not sure, he can ask the employee's advice. If it's halfway relevant, Junior will gamble on it. Same as you do. It's called letting nature take its course. Isn't that easier than fooling around with seminars, even if they are on a cruise boat?

Some owners worry whether their sons are old enough, or have enough schooling to take over.

"My boy is only 18, but he's out there pushing a crew." A contractor told me that with pride.

"My daughter wants to come in with me, but I insist she finish college first. Majoring in English. Learning to communicate." An electronics manufacturer offered that plan with even greater pride.

The myth that it's necessary for every young man or woman entering business to have a college degree has been so skillfully promoted by teachers and administrators that even some Independent Businessowners have bought it.

The fact that no college has the temerity to offer a course — much less a curriculum — in how to make money has been buried under the barrage of propaganda that a youngster "needs" a so-called liberal education to get along in the huge corporations that nobody really owns.

The unstated assumption that what is good for big business applies to independently owned enterprise has thus stolen four productive years from many a bright teenager.

Neither is there evidence that stockholders have received higher dividends as a result of corporations hiring the liberally educated, nor have any two pedagogues ever agreed on a definition of the term.

Following the adage to look for who benefits commercially or financially from any high-sounding endeavor, we find armies of teachers, administrators, and schoolbook publishers profiting by the parental gullibility and sacrifice that overloads campuses. Plus the inevitable politicians who skim a little off the top.

While a newcomer to your industry might benefit from some basic courses in drafting, accounting, electrical circuitry, computer programming, strength of materials, or whatever, the idea that college requires four years has no connection with anything today. Goes back to the Middle Ages.

In four wars, the education establishment sold our politicians the cruel concept that the life of a student was worth more than that of a soldier. Accordingly, their selling job is more intense now then ever, because without a war to induce young men to stay out of combat by staying in school, the younger generation is showing progressively less enthusiasm for a pupil's life after reaching the age of having better things to do.

Even if the purposes of large companies are served by hiring university graduates, your business is different. It's there to make a true profit — not a track record for a corporate bureaucrat. Your son or daughter can learn the business only by working at it.

The important question is whether Junior has the inherent sense of money that you have. Mechanics, engineers, accountants, and other technicians can be hired if the owner — whether he started, bought, or inherited the business — has the sense to buy low, sell high, fire drones, and keep expenses down.

Nothing to do with school. Many men without formal educations—Henry Ford and Henry Kaiser, to name two—built magnificent industries, and we have all seen countless "well-educated" derelicts. Some are called Professors of Business Administration.

Not to say you shouldn't buy your son a four-year vacation if you feel generous and he strongly desires it. But if he doesn't, and wants to get into business now, welcome him with open arms!

Your son's situation is unique. He has a job. Not to be confused with that of the individual who has to look for any job he can get. So the excuse that drinking, carousing, and demonstrating for four years will help get a job is irrelevant.

Four years out, the contractor's son will be able to run the family business for six months without guidance. At the same time, his contemporary who went to college—even if he studied Civil Engineering—will not know how to push a crew. And may have been conditioned to spend his life at the drawing board. While the young lady who probably already "communicates" effectively, must still learn the business.

There are as many ways of bringing your son to the heart of the business as there are owners. Here is one illustration:

Oscar, who was accumulating a chain of plating shops, asked me how to transfer authority to his son, Ajax.

The situation was this:

Oscar was getting along nicely doing cadmium and copper plating at his shop when the owner of a parallel enterprise in the next town died. Oscar bought that outfit from the widow, installed one of his mechanics as manager, and visited him every few days.

Some months later, a third shop came on the market, and within a few years Oscar—and his bank—owned five plants.

Several other men invested in the business, and Oscar found himself President of a growing corporation. They opened more establishments.

Oscar developed a reasonable set of controls, and functioned with the instincts of an Independent Businessowner. While all this was happening, Ajax grew up, got a degree in Business

Administration, and became first a production worker and later office manager in the business.

While Oscar had no problems permitting managers to run shops, and checking their work, something prevented him from turning the business over to Ajax.

The solution, as in many cases, resided in identifying the problem. It was that while he instinctively knew Ajax had a feel for a buck as well as for female employees, Oscar had confused day-to-day operations of a shop with managing the entire company.

My basic question to him was, "What do you do all day, Oscar?"

After several sessions of close questioning—Ajax participating—we identified 35 different duties he performed. Each was noted on a 3x5 card, which were then arranged into the following categories: Sales, personnel, purchasing, inventory control, merchandising and finance.

On each card, Oscar himself wrote Now, 60 days, 90 days, Joint-90 days, Joint-6 months, or Never. The last category temporarily bewildered both men, but I insisted it be there to spotlight the fundamental difference between managing a plating shop and operating the company that owns it.

These notes meant that Ajax was to assume the indicated responsibility now, in 30, 60 or 90 days, or work closely with Oscar for three to six months before assuming it.

There would be no point—nor have we space—to reproduce all 35 cards, but here are a few examples.

| Finance | Bank relationships | Never |
| | OK payment of bills | 60 days |
| Personnel | Scheduling employee hours | Now |
| | Hiring | 30 days |
| | Salary Reviews | 6 months |
| Purchasing | Commodities | 90 days |

Did it work? Almost. Sometimes Oscar "backslid," and undercut Ajax by acceding to a plant manager's request for a change of shift or a day off. On several occasions, I was called back for another three-way session.

The transition was 90 percent completed in less than six months. At that time, the company was given an opportunity to acquire another related business, and Oscar took it over. Ajax is on his tail for that now, too. And he's dealing with the bank.

Try something like this.

Basically, nepotism is just as important to owners as the principle of inheritance is to the jobholding population.

It underlies continuity of employment. An owner who cannot give or bequeath his business to offspring, with the opportunity to learn to run it, must sell or liquidate. In spite of newsworthy "mergers" — and I'll blow that silly idea out of the water in the next chapter — comparatively few businesses are salable. Those that are sold as often as not fall apart under new ownership, and liquidations throw people out of work.

I mention this only for the benefit of that small number of SOB's who might have some residual guilt about the situation, or question whether they are discharging a vague social obligation by taking over a business started by the previous generation.

Businessowners in some ways act as if they think they are kings. Have a regular dynastic complex. Start to worry about the question of succession as soon as the enterprise has barely taken root. This means they are anxiously evaluating the money-sense potential of their children — daughters are now in the picture as well as sons — because they know perfectly well that comparatively few jobholders could succeed them. Fully understand that anyone capable of owning a business would be doing so instead of working.

If you know that your kids obviously aren't going to make it as Businessowners, your only salvation is to sell or liquidate now. You do a son an injustice to keep him there as an ordinary employee, for he might be successful elsewhere.

As I said earlier, many SOB's are incapable of taking over the business, but seldom because they have conformed to the movie caricature of a stupid, lazy, or corrupt boss's son.

Usually these people have worked hard and are intelligent. The problem is that they don't have your peculiar instinct for money. As I said back at the beginning of this romp, in addition to dedication to the business, etc., the quality that sets you apart is the indefinable sense of money, the sense of timing, if you will, as to when to buy and when to sell. Not everybody has it.

If after reasonable exposure, the second generation is clearly cut out to be an employee — even at a high level in some organization — rather than an owner, you have no choice but to help him do it.

On the other hand, when the younger generation shows the business instinct, the future is bright for all concerned and the little ditty at the beginning of this chapter falls into place. A young man's physical energy and enthusiasm coupled with a father's experience has produced some powerful results in many firms. They are both lucky and happy.

Occasionally we get questions about conflicts between or among brothers in a family business. It is impractical for the father to arbitrate because after he's no longer there, fighting will resume. So if you have more than one son, decide early in the game whether the dominant one can handle the business and his brothers. If there is any doubt in your mind, then sell or liquidate as I'll describe in Chapter XV. Otherwise, after you're dead, the boys will fight, and the outfit will go downhill and fall apart.

Unless the son is a mean, aggressive SOB in the original sense, he is not going to get control of the business if the father resists.

Most of you talk a good game, but when push comes to shove, don't really want to give up control. For this reason, if you son has inherited any of your strengths, expect him to be as rough as you are.

A popular, deluded scenario we see over and over again is that of the father insisting, and the son actually believing that the son should work in all departments before making any business decisions. This is based on the unstated assumption that in order to run a business it's necessary to have personal experience in every corner of it. Nonsense.

Very few Businessowners meet this requirement themselves. For example, a pharmacist who builds a drug chain concludes he knows all phases of the business simply because he ran a store and knew how to count pills from a large bottle into a small one. In his chain, however, he has to employ people of various skills that he knows little about. Traffic management. Inventory control. Accounting. Advertising. Security. Store location. Store layout, and decor. The founder is not experienced in everything, so why should he require his son or daughter to work at all these jobs that have little to do with the decisions involved in buying, selling, hiring and firing?

A machinist who builds a manufacturing company, an electrician who does it in a service business, or a carpenter who now heads a construction firm, may all employ craftsmen or professionals from one another's trades. Yet he does not have a journeyman card in each of them, much less a university degree in the various fields.

Also, it is quite normal to find Businessowners with the meagerest notions of accounting, plant layout, advertising, or marketing. Usually they are, however, pretty good personal salesmen.

In view of the fact that the owner is making good money as a businessman whose background happened to be one particular field or another, what reason can there be for insisting that Junior "go through all the ropes"?

This may be related to the fact that human beings remain babies much longer than other animals. Especially true in the United States where people go to college full-time deep into their twenties, supported by their own parents or by all the parents of the United States through taxes.

Professional courses have been padded and spread out over a period of years in an obvious effort to minimize the number of new entrants into the respective fields. There is no evidence that a young fellow should spend four years reading nonsense before going to law school, and plenty of physicians and dentists after a few martinis admit their performance is in no way related to the undergraduate courses in everything under the sun they were required to sleep through.

Another objection to the notion that Junior should know the basic trade of the business is that the senior member of the outfit is usually so out of touch with changes in technology, that his early experience has no relevance to the buying, selling, hiring and firing which are the elements of making money. Trade knowledge gets old fast.

If an SOB is a lucky boy, it's not because he was born with a golden spoon in his mouth, because the government and competition can take that from him quickly. The reason he's lucky is he has a chance to get to the heart of the business — again, to the basic buying, selling, hiring, and firing functions — at an early age, and can sharpen these essential skills much faster than if he had to spend twenty years going from one boring job to another in a large company.

There is a great deal to be said for starting on a much higher level than your contemporaries. The head of a business he has inherited, who has done a good job by the time he's 40 should outclass anyone in the field.

He has to develop steel fast. No young man coming into his father's business can start firing people too soon. If he wants to be loved, he should become a professional lover, not a businessowner.

# CHAPTER FIFTEEN

# When Your Name is off the Door

Independent Businessowners who say they don't expect to live forever, sign conventional wills written by lawyers, and buy life insurance.

The trap awaiting these Independent Businessowners is that they act as if they really do expect to live forever, or at least until they are able to make orderly disposition of their businesses, according to their own plans. There's an old saying, "Man proposes; God disposes."

That these Businessowners have forgotten that is revealed by their failure to have written a business will.

You must write it yourself. No lawyer can write it for you. Hard to do, because it brings you closer to the unpleasant idea of your own death than paying an insurance premium or signing a will written by a lawyer. He is often a friend, and in spite of your discussions — usually concluded over lunch — there is nothing in the atmosphere to suggest you are really going to die.

A business will is a letter to the person designated to clean up after you, explaining the important matters you're working on, your options or alternatives for dealing with problems, etc. It also suggests — not orders! — who should do what, pending the final disposition of the business by sale, bequest, or liquidation.

Some people — surprisingly, women more than men — expect to run their businesses from the grave, by insisting that their wills include various hobbling provisions as to what may and may not be done. Such provisons are usually an unintentional, but legally enforceable prescription for bankruptcy.

If you have trouble writing your business will — and, incidentally, you'll learn a lot about your business by doing so — engage an outsider to ask you all of the questions that should be answered. Update the document every six months.

WHAT TO INCLUDE:

Financial: Who you're dealing with at the bank. History and nature of the relationship. What the banker understands to be your plans for repaying your loan. Where the money is to come from, and the payments schedule.

Purchasing: Key suppliers. Who you deal with in each firm. History and nature of relationships.

What factor to apply to their shipping promises and price firmness. Understandings covering shipments during the next six months. Alternative sources of supply.

Personnel: Strengths and weaknesses of supervisory employees. Amount of authority each can handle. Authority means making decisions and acting without asking anyone else's permission. Commitments — direct or implied — made to any employees regarding wages, salaries, benefits.

Who you deal with in the union. History and nature of relationship. Unresolved grievances, solutions to which could constitute major precedents. Understandings with labor officials, other businessowners, and industrial relations executives of large firms in the area concerning next round of negotiations.

Quality Control and Shipping: Weaknesses you know about, and plans to correct them.

Sales and Marketing: History and nature of relationship

with key accounts. How you ascertain what customers will want six and twelve months out. Programs for keeping salesmen or representatives sharp regarding both product knowledge and sales techniques. Weakness of various salesmen and how each are to be babied. Relationship with advertising agencies, and what you have in mind for next six months.

Competition: Strengths and weaknesses of principal competitors. Minor competitors showing promise of becoming major.

The above are illustrative, and should serve as thoughtstarters to help you begin to answer the questions that your unprepared successor should ask.

Businessowners who have done this, and think that the worst thing that could happen to their business is their own premature death, have deliberately excluded from their thoughts on planning and preparations the equally inadmissable idea of their prolonged disability. Alive, but not able to make decisions.

I've seen owners who are obviously not clear in their minds owing to the effects of illness and medicines, attempting to second guess everything done in the business from a hospital or convalescent home.

Result: Gradual reduction in profitability, then losses, then bankruptcy. Too late in these proceedings, conservatorships are sometimes arranged. By that time there is nothing much left to conserve.

Death has some advantages as far as the business is concerned. It is a clear-cut situation. It's obvious that somebody has to take charge.

But if you're backed up into the hospital or seriously ill at home, with people running back and forth trying to get permission to do things, or sugar-coating bad problems while at the same time trying to get your best judgment as to what to do about them, your instructions or advice will be directly proportional to the accuracy of your information and the quality of your thinking.

The most difficult, unnatural thing for any Businessowner

to do is to give up authority. Hard enough under ordinary conditions, but infinitely more excruciating if incapacitated. And that's when it's most important to do so.

### WHAT TO DO:

1.   Now, while you're OK, add a "codicil" to that business will, appointing a committee with the steadiest member of your immediate family as Chairman, with authority to decide that an emergency exists and that decision-making authority must be given to the person you have designated. Include your lawyer, CPA, and any trusted friend who might understand something about the business.

Include a management or business consultant only if you know him well, have used his services before, and believe that he has the knowledge and ability to make a measurable contribution.

The legal details — temporary or permanent conservatorship, guardianship, etc. — are less important than selecting the right man to run things, or sell or liquidate your business if it doesn't look like you'll get back in time to put it together again.

2.   Decide right now who should take over this afternoon if you should get into a wreck coming back from lunch. A crash that will take you out of the picture for many months.

Attach this "codicil" to your business will, with instructions for it to be opened by a designated individual in the event of your death or disability. Give copies to your spouse and lawyer.

How do you establish accountability? Probably you can't but this individual's compensation should be tied to the business's profits while he is in charge. Prepare that plan now.

In some cases it will make sense to specify who, in your family, this emergency General Manager should report to. Also, it might be wise to arrange for your spouse or other responsible family member to be the only person authorized to sign checks.

Also — tomorrow morning! — show this individual how to spot any salary increases in the payroll. We're assuming that paychecks are produced by a computer service, or are at least machine-signed in your office.

3.   Review this matter every ninety days in case you want to change the name of the emergency Manager. Even if he is your son. No reason to tell this individual in advance that he has been so named. Sometimes it's best not to.

Even if the man you have elected makes mistakes — and he will — it's better than not making decisions at all because of not having authority.

Now you're becoming more convinced that you're not going to live forever and that you can't run your business from the grave.

You face the question who takes over next on a non-emergency basis. What are your options? How do you decide? And how to accomplish the transition?

It was inevitable that this matter was introduced to some degree in the previous chapter concerning SOB's. Now we're looking at the broader picture — all of your options for the long haul.

First, get the horse in front of the cart, instead of the reverse, which is usually the case. I refer to what publicists for the legal and accounting fraternities call "tax angling." Some of these worthies have Businessowners so terrified of the tax collector that they think about the tax consequences of a transaction before they know what the transaction is.

As in other matters, it is your job as owner to decide what to do. Then tell your lawyer and accountant to do it legally. If you ask them whether you can do it, the answer of course will be no. And if you tell them what to do and they say they can't do it, well, the yellow pages are full of other lawyers and accountants.

Ascertain the tax consequences of each option only after you've listed them in order of economic and personal benefits.

In deciding who should take over next, the Businessowner is normally under the influence of two hang-ups. First is how you got into the game. Did you start from scratch? Buy the business? Inherit?

Don't assume that whoever takes over after you is going to

have the same point of view you had when you began. Don't try to imagine the other fellow's attitude or state of mind. This is basically a financial, not a psychological matter.

The other hang-up that gets in the way of straight business thinking in this situation has to do with your wishes — with what you want to do. You can seldom do what you want to do. You do what you can, what the market will permit you to do.

For example, you may wish to sell the business, but there's no buyer. You may prefer that your son take over, but he's incapable of or not interested in doing so.

So what are your alternatives?

You only have three choices. You can make a gift of or bequeath the business, liquidate, or sell it. Some people like to say "sell or merge," and I'll eviscerate that merger idea shortly.

Obviously the most popular choice of the Businessowner who has children is gradually to give them the business in accordance with tax regulations and will them the remainder. This is not only good economic sense when it can work, but good psychology. Fits the comfortable dynastic urge that I mentioned in the last chapter. The modern, industrial version of having children so they can support you in your old age. Whether they actually do so is another matter.

Now it's time to recapitulate to some extent and re-emphasize a few of the points in the last chapter in order to lead into all the options you have and how to deal with them.

In giving in to this dynastic urge, remember a theme that goes throughout this book, which is that the quality that sets you apart is your ability to translate events into dollars. Fast. Without conscious calculation. The money-sense or instinct. You go for return on investment the way a carnivore goes for the jugular.

And, as I've been saying, this cannot be conveyed. You can send your son to college and he can learn engineering, agriculture, horticulture, personnel management, chemistry, and even accounting. But no college can teach him to make money, or inculcate the money sense. Colleges and universities don't offer courses in this subject.

Obviously, if one got a professor who discovered he could give one, he would quit teaching and apply his talents elsewhere to reap the rewards thereof. So, not only do colleges not teach such courses, but they never will be able to.

The question arises, how to decide whether Junior has the money-sense. A more formal writer would have insisted on covering the matter in the previous chapter but it's really only one alternative available to you when you are deciding what to do with the business.

In most cases, all you really know is that Junior is a hard worker and has done a good job wherever you have put him. He's never made a truly business decision. You have to find out whether he can. So does he. You also know whether he has tried to push you out of the picture. If not, he's in trouble. If Sonny has given you the same respect, and deferred to you as he did when he was a little boy at home, chances are he doesn't have what it takes. Further, the more rebellious teenager he was, the more likelihood he'll fight you in the business. If he's always been a nice boy, chances are he's not worth much.

The expression, "management succession," implies no change of ownership.

The notion belongs where it originated — in the large, public corporations that nobody really owns and frequently nobody really runs. The independently owned business by definition, structure, and purpose is the function of a single individual who either has what it takes or goes down in flames.

Fact is that management succession in the independently owned business is impossible without ownership succession.

If you say that your son practically runs the business now — and remember, there's a whale of a difference between running a business (deciding what to do), and administering it (getting it done) — give him the business now.

Or, if you must, sell it to him on practical economic, tax, and family grounds. Don't wait to bequeath it to him.

Don't be like the well-known founder and chief executive of a large company who was still firmly entrenched at 75. His son, 50, one day asked him when he planned to retire.

"Never," growled the old man. "Then how about me retiring?" responded the son.

Work things out with the CPA and lawyer before tax laws get any more restrictive. If Junior has demonstrated any effort to steal your job and push you out, in any of the ways that I mentioned in the last chapter or with better techniques he thought up, give him the business right now. Also the top title (do not make him "President" and yourself "Chairman"), and the fancy office. Expect him to fire your secretary, who has been torturing him for 22 years, and hire a better-looking one of his own.

You may experience mixed emotions, as if watching your mother-in-law drive your new Cadillac over a cliff, but it's the only way to learn what you need to know.

Work out a system for transferring your duties to him, similar to the one outlined in the last chapter or a better one that you devise. Make this a real transfer of responsibility and authority.

Then ask the young man for a job as consultant, but don't show up too often. Remember, the only power a consultant has is the power of persuasion. Recognize early in your new career as counselor that clients buy more advice than they follow.

Regarding your income, considering the years you've put in, if the business can't provide enough for both of you, it probably should be sold or liqudated anyway.

The reason to play out this scenario is for both of you to find out whether Junior can really make money running a business. You didn't know whether you had the ability to do so until you tried. Faced the possibility of bankruptcy and loss of self-respect if you failed. Junior needs to have a lot to lose, which, as I pointed out before, is at least half the owner's motivation.

If Junior can't hack it, there's still time to sell him the idea — if he hasn't already reached the same conclusion — of saving what he can by selling to one of the prospects you lined up during your leisurely career as a consultant, when you were not underfoot all the time in your son's business. That's what you were up to when you weren't interfering in the plant, office, store, or whatever.

What about the liquidation option? When do you do it? Obviously when you have nobody to take over and there is no likely buyer for the business in its present form. Or, better yet, even if you do have an heir who looks OK, and you can get more for the business dead than alive.

Sometimes a company is sitting on real estate, equipment or raw material that can command a greater price than what it can earn. Only the market determines these things. Obviously real estate is, or at least traditionally has been, the principal asset that could make it more attractive to liquidate a business than to keep it going — under any ownership or management.

If the business is doing well, this is a painful decision. Requires much self-discipline. Even though you or your son might want to stay and work, if all economic factors point to liquidation as the most rational course, do it and cry all the way to the bank.

Now at last we come to that never-never land of mergers. Let's define a few terms. The expression "merger" implies a condition which seldom exists — that two companies of equal size are being made into one.

For practical purposes, few so-called mergers meet this test. The expression is deceiving. The truth is that there are sell-outs and take-overs. If you read the *Wall Street Journal* carefully when mergers are described, you'll find that there is usually a "surviving company." Means that one company did not survive.

Accordingly, it is psychologically important that you get it clearly into your head that you're not likely to merge the business. You might sell it. If so, it will be taken over, and its identity rightfully destroyed. That's part of your identity. Face it.

Whether you are getting cash, stock, or a combination thereof, it is necessary to prepare for the negotiation the same way athletes train for a big event. Preparation consists of getting one basic idea into your head and carrying out fifteen steps.

The basic idea is that you're not selling a business but an opportunity for the other fellow to acquire untold wealth. There is a bit of the con-man in this, which may be hard for most Businessowners. Chances are that by nature you are a square shooter dealing in tangibles. But you have to sell the intangible idea that you regrettably have to give up this opportunity for all the riches of Araby if you're going to make a deal.

As a corollary, you require a plausible reason for unloading. Age. Health. Your wife's health. You want to travel. Lack the energy or resources to build the business up to its true potential.

Whatever the reason, make sure it can be expressed in a way that makes sense to someone else who has probably bought quite a few businesses. That's another tricky point in all this. You will only sell a business once, but if you sell to a large company, they've bought a lot of them and know a few tricks that may not have occurred to you.

What are the fifteen steps?

1.  Pay down debt. Sacrifice current opportunities to have a reasonable debt structure.

2.  As a corollary to #1, do everything possible to build the balance sheet. You want the strongest possible current ratio for your industry. And, as indicated in #1, the most attractive debt to equity ratio.

3.  Accumulate cash. Stint yourself on inventory, but build cash. Cash to a prospective buyer is as honey to bees.

4.  You need a CPA audit, preferably for at least three years by the same CPA firm. It's amazing how many substantial, independently owned businesses have never been required by their banks or insurance companies to have a CPA audit. As a result the owners have had no incentive to spend the money. It is essential, however, to have such a report if you hope to get a good price for the business.

5.    Clean up any actual or pending litigation, regardless how trivial. When larger companies are looking at smaller ones, their legal staffs quite rightly are concerned about contingent liabilities. Sure, they might just buy your assets instead of your corporation, but still don't care to take chances.

6.    By the same token, clean up any current or pending problems with regulatory agencies, especially regarding environmental and fair employment matters. The potential contingent liabilities in these areas are terrifying.

7.    Clean up anything that may suggest questionable ethics or improprieties. Be very harsh with yourself. Personal expense accounts, for example. Yachts. Hunting lodges.

8.    Don't start new programs. For example, a new plant, building, or whole new product line. Also opening of additional sales offices. Fine to have all these things on the drawing boards. The more extensive a smorgasbord of potentially profitable programs you have designed and have ready to go, the more attractive is the business.

9.    Obtain a complete market survey, showing what you control and what competition is doing. Truthfully. Develop a program to increase your market share which might require the strength of a larger company. Sales records must include product line profitability.

10.    If you have a union, start to sell right after a contract has been signed. If it will take a couple of years to complete the transaction, consider buying an extra year or two from the union, even at cost of higher wages. Acquiring companies don't like to start with labor problems.

11.    If you own the real estate personally, get advice whether to sell it with the business or lease to the buyer. A matter of negotiations of course, but you must know where you stand.

12.    Have competent people at the foreman level. Chances are that so-called management and staff employees will be replaced. OK to show weakness in that area. Inviting to some overstaffed, acquisition-minded companies.

13.    Don't consider your employees. Regardless what pro-

mises are made by the negotiator for the buyer that they will not fire your favorite old-timers, etc., it just won't wash when the actual new manager arrives. A new broom sweeps very clean in these circumstances. If you feel you owe something to an employee, give him a bonus the day before the transfer is accomplished. Many Businessowners have needlessly left money on the table thinking they were buying something for "their guys."

14.    Use outside help both in preparing to negotiate and in actually negotiating for the sale of your business. You are bound to be emotional, and need disinterested guidance to keep you on an even keel.

In any negotiation — for real estate, in collective bargaining, or selling a business — the cards you hold mean nothing. The cards the other fellow thinks you hold mean everything. This important difference is blurred to anyone emotionally involved in the situation.

15.    As to asking price, value is what you can persuade the buyer he can earn in the future. Practice creating pro forma statements showing how more money can be made. As I said earlier, you are not offering a static business, but an opportunity for riches beyond imagination!

Selling a business is like selling a home. You have to clean it up first. Legally, financially, and operationally. For the first two areas, obviously you need a lawyer and a CPA both for preparing to negotiate and in actual negotiating.

Often, the old family retainer type of lawyer is useless. He might know all about wills and real estate and getting Junior out of the poogie when he wrecks the family car, but has no experience in cleaning up a business to sell or protecting you in the final contract. Don't buy him an education.

The same is true to a lesser degree of CPA's. An individual practitioner would not be up to date on all aspects of a situation like this. You don't need to go to one of the Big Eight firms, but do need an outfit that has a couple of partners who have previously been involved in the sale of businesses.

How do you find out whether these professionals have had

the requisite experience? Ask them. Then visit the clients they refer you to and get their opinion. Like hiring other types of high priced help. Investigate references carefully, in person. Check with other former owners who sold out, and ascertain who they used. If you go elsewhere for this expertise and your old lawyer and accounting pals from the Chamber of Commerce or the Country Club are unhappy, that's the way life is. Tell them that they win a few and lose a few.

Regarding consultants. This breed of cat is sometimes more experienced in actual negotiations than CPA's and attorneys. The reason is that many of us have been through it ourselves, and got into consulting by virtue of being asked to help other people sell their businesses. But check them out carefully.

Accordingly, it is entirely possible that you might use all three professionals in this transaction, and it could be well worth the money. Again, it's the experience of the individuals not their firms, that is important. Ask specific questions.

How to judge an offer from a larger company?

Depends on which of three possible situations you have in mind.

1. You will receive cash on barrelhead and escape with it.

2. You will accept part or all payment in stock and get out.

3. You will accept part or all in stock and remain.

In situation #1, the only question is whether the bank will certify the buyer's check.

In situation #2, there is the matter of the check, and also their dividend records. That's all you can go by. Don't try to outguess the stock market.

In situation #3, you are looking at their dividend record plus a few other little matters.

Why do they want to buy your company? To whom will you report? How do you know? How long has he been with the company? Will it function as an independent entity or will it be dismembered into the various departments of the buying company? What will your job really be? Will you actually run your former company as a separate entity, responsible only to make a profit? To what extent will you be governed by staff of the parent company?

Where do you get answers to these questions? From other former Businessowners who have sold out to the same company. And from no other source.

The longer your name has been on the door the lower the probability you will be successful as an employed politician in the business you used to own.

So if Junior does not take it over, and your name is off the door, the game is over. Lose no sleep wondering whether you've done the right thing. Beat it. Scram. You're through.

Move on to the next stage of your life with eagerness, enthusiasm, and the expectation that "the best is yet to be."

Don't look back.

* * * END * * *

# Index

Affirmative Action Program (AAP), 144, 145, 146
AFL-CIO, 12, 51, 65, 126
American Management Association, 152
Anspacher, Carolyn, 185

balance of payments, 75-76, 77
*Barron's*, 82
Benson, Herbert, 147
Brazil, 92
Bretton Woods monetary conference, 73

Carter, Jimmy, 75, 142
Chessman, Caryl, 185
Chrysler, 27, 43, 48, 54, 128
Civil Rights Act, 145
continuing education 151-61
Control Data, 7
credit crunch, 96-98

Dale, Edwon L, Jr., 93
depression, 73-74, 95
*Dow Theory Letter*, 176

Eisenhower, Dwight, 129, 163
employees:
    firing, 223-35
    hiring, 179-91
    treatment, 193-221
*Enterprise*, 11
Equal Employment Opportunity Commission (EEOC), 144, 145, 146, 147
Equitable Life, 14
exchange rates, 72-73, 74
Exxon, 129

Fair Labor Standards Act, 67, 218
Federal Reserve, 77-78, 79, 93, 94
fixed exchange rates, 72-73, 74
floating exchange rates, 72-73
*Forbes*, 155
Ford Foundation, 53, 54
Ford, Henry, I, 13, 15, 244
Ford, Henry, II, 15

General Motors, 27, 129
gold, 72-73, 96

*Harvard Business Review*, 53
Hill, Napoleon, 160
Hoover, Herbert, 75

IBM, 55, 56, 128
industrial relations, 56
interest rates, 76-77

investment, 81-87

Jack & Heintz, 213
Johnson, Lyndon Baines, 75, 144

Kaiser, Henry, 242
Keynesian economics, 77, 91, 93
Kodak, 55, 56

Labor Department, 145
labor unions, 51-69
Lincoln Electric Welding, 213
Lincoln, John C., 213
Lockheed, 43, 48

Madden, Carl H., 11, 13, 14
McDonald Douglas Corporation, 60
Meany, George, 26
Muskie, Senator, 129

National Association of Corporate
    Directors, 101
National Labor Relations Board,
    133
*Nation's Business*, 155
*New York Times*, 93
*Newsletters for Independent
    Businessowners* (NIB), 58
Nixon, Richard, 72, 96

Office of Federal Contract Compliance
    Programs (OFCCP), 144,
    145, 146

OSHA, 14-15, 131

Peale, Norman Vincent, 160
Penn Central, 43, 48
Proposition 13, 15

recession, 73-74, 95
*Relaxation Response, The*
    (Benson),
Rockwell, Al, 13
Rogers, Will, 151
Roosevelt, Franklin Delano, 52, 55,
    77, 91, 93, 163
Rukeyser, Louis, 135, 136, 186
Russell, Richard, 176

Salton, Inc., 104-5
Salton, Lewis, 104-5
*San Francisco Chronicle*, 185
Schrank, Robert, 53-54

*Time*, 14
Truman, Harry, 6, 163-64

unions, 51-69
*U.S. News*, 155

wage-price controls, 144
Wagner Act, 52
*Wall Street Journal*, 59, 90, 129,
    154, 155
Williams, John D., 134
Wolfe, Thomas, 183

Earl D. Brodie has earned the right to do this book—In business from the age of 14, he eventually joined his father in the Brodie Meter Company, which he took public and finally merged with Rockwell International. During those years he did everything one does in a medium-sized manufacturing business. He became President of the California Metal Trades Association; is a Founding Member of the Institute of Management Consultants; and a Charter Member of the National Speakers Association. Now, as Management Consultant he has served over 100 clients and has addressed more than 300 business audiences. He is also Editor and Publisher of the widely-read Newsletter For Independent Businessowners.

"Recently a beautiful ad by Control Data was headed "The Business of Business is to Address the Major Needs of Society."

That may be the business of Control Data, but it is exactly the opposite of the business of the Independent Businessowner, and the extent that he believes such claptrap, he is economically castrating himself.

Just among us businessowners, let's admit that the purpose of your business is to provide as high a standard of living and as much security as possible for yourself and those dependent upon you. Now, if you want to label making and selling drill presses, or merchandising candy bars and toothpaste, to machine shops or drugstore customers as addressing a major need of society, go to it. But if you do, remember that's a private joke.

The major threat to the independent businessowner is the mistaken idea that he has any purpose of being in business other than to make some dough. Now, after you've made your money, if you want to donate it to the Society for Homeless Goldfish or to any other worthy cause, that's your business. It's your dough and you can do what you want with it, but don't get that confused with the whole point of being in business.

If you're looking for a book of standard forms or procedures, the library is full of them. We're less concerned with how to do things than we are with the principal question of the businessowner, which is what to do. Besides, telling others how to do things is usually a waste of energy. The main objective is to be sure that businessowners know what to do. Once that's clearly in mind—and by the normal course of events through the owner's head and into the heads of employees—the "how" part comes easy.

The purpose of this book is to enable the Independent Businessowner to see himself correctly as the unique individual that he is—philosophically,